BLACK FRIDAY COMING DOWN

BLACK FRIDAY COMING DOWN

DAVID HUNTER

RUTLEDGE HILL PRESS
Nashville, Tennessee

Published in Nashville, Tennessee, by Rutledge Hill Press,
513 Third Avenue South, Nashville, Tennessee 37210

Typography by Bailey Typography, Nashville, Tennessee

Library of Congress Cataloging-in-Publication Data

Hunter, David, 1947–
    Black Friday coming down / David Hunter.
        p.   cm.
    ISBN 1-55853-061-4
    1. Hunter, David, 1947–   . 2. Police—Tennessee—Knoxville—
Biography. I. Title.
HV7911.H825A3   1990
363.2'092—dc20   89-70361
    [B]   CIP

Printed in the United States of America
1 2 3 4 5 6 7 8 — 96 95 94 93 92 91 90

Contents

Introduction

The response to my first book, *The Moon Is Always Full,* has overwhelmed me. I am a private person not given to public displays of emotion. Accepting praise is difficult for me. There is no false modesty involved when I try to steer attention from myself to my books. A book, after all, is a living entity, independent even of the author.

No matter how wonderful the response to a book, though, a writer cannot linger. Writers write. Those who cease to do so become former writers, pitifully trying to stand on past accomplishments.

Although *Black Friday Coming Down* is similar to my first book, the two books are not the same. I am still a cop in love with the profession. My idealism is still intact—a little more battered, but alive and well—I have not lost the belief that cops are special people deserving of a voice from within the ranks to plead their case and define their problems.

Not even the universe, however, can resist the forces acting upon it. Given time, a small stream of water carves out the Grand Canyon and the ocean pounds the shore into granules of sand.

A little more melancholia, perhaps, oozes from between the lines of this book than from the last. I have been in courtrooms a hundred times since it was written, watching lawyers work their alchemy until words such as *truth* and *justice* become lost in the sophistry of the barristers' art.

Since finishing the first book, I have seen people die and I have held infants in my arms; I have laughed and I have cried; I have loved and I have hated. I have watched a few more precious days of my life pass away. Nothing stands still; nothing escapes change.

There are new subjects, new people in *Black Friday Coming Down*. There are also some old subjects, one of them being the concept of evil. To me, evil is more than a theological abstraction. I have been toe to toe with it. In a chapter called "The Bad Seed," I explore another facet of the subject.

Humor, laughter, and irony are still to be found in great quantities, sometimes in unexpected places. Laughter, after all, is the cop's greatest ally in fending off the demons lurking about him.

This book, like the first, is true. There are still difficulties, however, inherent in writing about real people. The names of nonpolice personnel have been changed. Where requested, the names of cops have been altered. Times, places, and frequency of arrest have been changed so that individuals cannot be tracked down through records. There are composites.

Still, I say to you, this book is true. The pain, the joy, the weeping, and the laughing—they all are true.

And once again I must say, "These particular stories took place in Knoxville, Tennessee. You can substitute the name of any American city, however. It does not matter."

The human condition is universal.

BLACK
FRIDAY
COMING
DOWN

1

"Tell Millie I'll Be Along Soon"

The faces of the people in the milling crowd told me it was not something I really wanted to see. At the scene of a minor accident, there will be laughter and joking. The spectators that night had the hopeless look of those who want to help but do not really want to touch the horror before them.

It was not even my jurisdiction, but you cannot pass up someone in trouble. Flipping on the blue lights, I got out with a sigh. Second shift was just beginning, and I had not even made it to my beat.

"He walked right out in front of me. Honest to God, I couldn't miss him!" The speaker had the wild, disheveled look of a man trying to wake up from a nightmare. He was John Q. Citizen, sober and on his way home. Fate had halted his progress, and he could not believe what had happened. Such things happen to other people, never to you.

"Stand over there," I told him, "until a city officer shows up to work the accident." Numbly he complied. I had no fear that he would try to flee.

The victim was on his back in the deep ditch, half sitting up against the embankment where he had landed. His legs were the first thing I noticed. They did not look like human limbs. Pretzellike, they were twisted around and together, the feet at odd angles to the body.

Then the face snapped into focus. The man, very old and frail, stared up at me as I approached. He was calm and resigned. As a child, I once watched a cat play with a mouse, until the mouse also became calm and resigned. Illogically, the memory flashed across my mind.

"Get an ambulance en route. Tell them to hurry," I said. "Also advise the city that I need an officer. I have a pedestrian down."

Kneeling beside him, I said one of those silly things that you always say when confronted with the specter of a mortally wounded individual. You say such things because there is nothing else you can say.

"Good evening, sir. Try to relax and be calm. The ambulance will be here in just a few minutes."

"No hurry, young man. I'm in no pain, whatsoever." His speech had the broad vowels of Ohio in it.

As he spoke, I saw the splinters of bone protruding from his shirt where the collar bone had torn through the flesh. First aid did not cross my mind. His injuries were too massive for my few hours of academy first aid training to even attempt anything. I did take off my windbreaker and cover him with it, though.

"Is there anything I can do for you, sir?"

"Yes, as a matter of fact there is. My Millie is back at the motel. I walked down looking for a newspaper. Could you go back up there and tell her I'll be along as soon as the doctors take a look at me?"

I took out my pad and wrote down the name and room number from the motel just up the street, more to give myself something to do than anything else. While I was writing, I did not have to look at his ruddy face, with lines like parchment around a mouth that had smiled a lot, or the white, wispy hair falling over his forehead.

"It's our fiftieth year in Knoxville," the old man said, "our anniversary. We were going to spend our honeymoon in New Orleans, but we never got that far. Millie fell in love with these hills as we drove through. You local folks don't know how lucky you are. This is one of the most beautiful places on earth." He coughed, and a slight pink foam appeared on his lips.

12

"Tell that ambulance to step it up," I snapped into the radio.

"You will be sure to go and tell Millie, won't you, officer? She worries about me. After fifty years, you begin to feel like there's only one person in the house. You get close."

"Yes, sir, I'll do it, or someone else will. You just relax now. Help is on the way."

A dread was already on me. I would knock on the motel door; a fragile woman with white hair would answer, a smile on her lips, expecting her husband of fifty years. I would have to tell her he had been hit by a car and was mutilated beyond belief.

"I know the driver must be upset. You tell him it wasn't his fault. I had other things on my mind and wasn't paying attention."

"I'll do that, sir."

"Do you have any children, officer?"

"Yes, sir, I do. Three of them. Two girls and a boy."

"Enjoy them," he said. "Enjoy them while you can. Millie and me had three, but one of them died of polio. Time passes quick. One day it'll be just you and your wife."

"Yes, sir, that's true. They grow up too fast."

He coughed again. Someone handed me a clean white handkerchief. I wiped the bloody froth from his lips. It seemed forever since I had arrived, but it had been only minutes.

"We once planned on retiring here, but the children settled near us and we never got around to leaving. I guess if you live here, the place loses some of its magic."

"No, sir, not really. I spend most of my vacations within thirty miles of here."

The incongruity of the situation overwhelmed me. A human being was dying inches from me, and we were discussing vacation spots. I wanted to throw back my head and howl like a wolf to relieve the pain that was washing through me. There is too much pain out there—and too much I've seen. *Dear Jesus*, I silently prayed, *please don't let me disgrace myself.*

It was as if the rest of the world had ceased to exist momentarily. There were no gawking spectators or cars creeping by, spectators hanging out ghoullike for a glance at blood and gore. The two of us were alone.

Then I heard the ambulance, siren yelping jerkily as the driver threaded through the crowd. A city police cruiser was right behind it.

Moments later, two young paramedics (they always seem young these days) had pushed me aside and were ministering to the old man in soft voices, with no hint of panic or emotion.

"You got any details?" the city officer asked, preparing to take notes.

"Over there's your driver," I pointed at the man, who was waving his arms, trying to persuade anyone who would listen that he could not have avoided turning the elderly man into a side of bloody meat. "The victim told me that he wasn't paying attention. He said it was his fault."

"Officer," one of the paramedics yelled, "this gentleman would like to speak to you before we move him."

The city officer and I jumped lightly into the ditch. I leaned over the man and the other paramedic handed me my windbreaker.

"Yes, sir?" I said.

"Officer, you've been very kind. Please be sure and tell Millie that I'll be along soon . . . when the doctors release me. I don't want her to worry."

The paramedic standing behind the old man looked at me and shook his head sadly.

"I'll do that, sir." I managed to control the catch in my throat.

As we climbed back out of the ditch, the dispatcher called me. A fight, or some other disturbance, had broken out on my beat. Relief flooded through me, and shame at the same time. I was relieved of the responsibility of talking to the old man's wife.

"Here's the room number and the name." I handed them to the city officer. "I have a call waiting."

"I'll take care of it," he said. "I'll see that she gets to the hospital."

"Thanks. I'll give you a holler after a while."

It was a busy shift, replete with domestic disturbances, auto accidents, and barroom brawls. The shift was almost over before I slipped back down the highway into the city looking for the officer who had worked the accident.

I was about to have my dispatcher call him to meet me when

14

I saw him backed into a closed business. His dome light on, he obviously was catching up on paperwork. He glanced up as I eased in beside him.

"Have you been as busy as I have tonight?" he asked.

"Things have been moving right along," I replied.

"The old man made it to the hospital, but he died before they even started to work on him. It was unbelievable how bad he was messed up, especially to be as alert as he seemed."

I only nodded.

"The doctor told me that the human body gives off its own painkiller. He definitely felt no pain right up to the end."

"How did his wife hold up?"

"Funny thing," the city officer said, "he was at the motel by himself. I made the clerk go over the list several times. From the hospital, we got hold of one of his sons. The son said his mother's been dead about twelve years—the old man drove down every year on their anniversary."

"Well, I appreciate it," I told him, then wheeled away quickly. I could not let another cop see what I knew was about to happen, what is happening even now as I write these words. My fellow officer appeared puzzled at my abrupt departure. The stinging tears did not break through until I was up the highway a mile or so.

I thought of the frail old man making his yearly pilgrimage alone for twelve years. He probably visited the places they had first visited as newlyweds. It brought her close to him again, I have no doubt.

The old man was right, you know. When you live with someone you love, after a while it's like there's only one person in the house. Your needs become her needs, your triumphs become hers. The two of you mesh into a unit stronger than either individual.

I pictured him leaving the motel, perhaps turning to tell her he would be right back, then remembering that she had been away for twelve years. After a while, I remembered his last message to her, the last one this side of the mystery.

There in the darkness of my cruiser I delivered that message aloud to a woman who had been dead twelve years, to a woman I had never met in this life. It did not seem odd at all.

"He'll be along soon, Millie. He just left here, and he'll be along soon."

Oh death, where is thy sting?

15

2

"Father, Forgive Me, For I Have Sinned"

On the evening of December 7, 1988, just a few minutes before eight o'clock, Officer Bob Wooldridge of the Knoxville, Tennessee, Police Department killed a man.

He had hoped that such a thing would never happen but, as with all street cops, he had lived with the horrible specter throughout his career. It was nothing at all like the movies.

At eight o'clock I was walking through the front doors of the *Knoxville News-Sentinel* for an interview when I met Miles Carey, a photographer for the *News-Sentinel*, hurriedly leaving the building.

"There's been an officer involved in a shooting on Jourolman Avenue," he said. "I don't know if we have an officer down or not!"

My first impulse was to jump in the cruiser and go to the scene. I knew that Bob Wooldridge, a close personal friend for years, was running that beat. Instead, I switched my radio from the sheriff's department frequency to the Knoxville police frequency. I knew there would be pandemonium at the scene, and I would only get in the way.

It soon became obvious that there would be no further information on the air. The lid was on, and communications were being kept to a minimum. I went to a phone and called the dispatcher, who told me that there had been a shooting, but no officer was down. Yes, Bob Wooldridge was the officer involved.

I was relieved, but still worried. The trauma of shooting another human being is almost as bad as being shot, and officers have a hard time coping with it.

When my interview was finished, I drove to the city police department. Of the two reporters waiting in the lobby, I recognized Maria Cornelius of the *News-Sentinel*.

"Do you know anything about this?" she asked.

"No more than you do. In fact, if you were at the scene, you know more than I do."

"Do you know Officer Wooldridge?"

"He's one of my closest friends. His Christmas present is under my tree right now."

"What can you tell me about him?"

"He's cool under pressure and one of the most professional officers I know. I've never seen him come apart under pressure."

Maria jotted down my words. Deadline was approaching, and it seemed unlikely there would be any further information before that time. Reporters have to make do with what they have.

As I talked to the reporters, two Knoxville Police Department officers got off the elevator. "Did you want to go up, Hunter?" one of them asked.

"Yeah, I thought I'd drive Bob home. I have to go north anyway."

"Come on, I'll take you up." A key is required to operate the elevator. The officer accepted my remark about "going north anyway," without comment. He knew that I was worried about Bob but that cops cannot admit to such ordinary human emotion.

In the criminal investigation offices, I saw patrolmen Charlie Newman and Don Jones slouching against a desk. Jones, a husky man with sandy hair and a mustache, had graduated from the police academy eighteen months earlier. Newman, a veteran officer with mischief in his eyes, is the kind of cop of whom supervisors say, "That Charlie is a good cop, but he needs to settle down." They mean he should curtail such activities as installing a miniature flashing Christmas tree on the dash of his car during the holidays.

After we talked about my book for a few minutes, as if it was the last thing on my mind, I casually asked what had happened. The officers, of course, were glad to explain.

The call had begun over an hour before the shooting when Bob responded to a complaint at a laundromat on Beaumont Avenue. The complainant, an Ohio resident, told Wooldridge that he was on his way home from a trip to Georgia. A passenger who had traveled to Georgia with him had gone berserk and kicked the windshield out, then fled the area. He did not want to file a report, he declared, but he did want the police to know that the man was on foot somewhere in the vicinity.

Near the intersection of Beaumont and Reed streets, Wooldridge spotted the suspect behaving in a bizarre manner, hurling himself on his back, kicking his legs, and screaming incoherently. Upon seeing the police cruiser, he fled. Wooldridge followed in the cruiser until the suspect darted into a fenced-in back yard. Wooldridge then continued on foot.

Bob Wooldridge is about five feet, eight inches tall and weighs in around 150 pounds. The suspect was approximately five feet, ten inches tall and around 170 pounds. The officer had intended to wait on back-up, having no intention of a one-on-one confrontation with the obviously disturbed suspect, but the choice was taken from him.

An elderly man and woman who came out on their front porch to see what was going on did not respond to Wooldridge's instructions to get back inside. Fearing for their safety, he went into their yard and got between them and the raving man.

Still screaming incoherently, the suspect grabbed a piece of angle iron in a small garden. It was about five feet long, with two feet of it underground, but the man pulled it up effortlessly and began swinging it over his head.

Wooldridge yelled for him to drop it, at least three times according to other officers and civilian witnesses. Then the man advanced, bringing the angle iron back to club the officer. A fraction of a second later, Wooldridge fired one round from his nine millimeter Sig-Sauer semiautomatic pistol, only recently approved for use by Knoxville officers.

The round hit the suspect dead center in the chest, the area that officers call "the kill zone." Bob would tell me later, "I don't remember drawing my weapon *or* aiming, it all happened so fast. They're right. You automatically do what you've been trained to do."

According to witnesses, the suspect bent forward slightly as the round hit him, then crumpled, dropping the angle iron. It was later announced that he had died at the hospital. The officers knew better. He had died where the round stopped him.

Wooldridge stood, weapon in hand, staring at the downed suspect until another officer came up and told him to put the weapon away. A few minutes later, shiftmate Carl Jenkins, a big, blond bear of a man, had Wooldridge sitting in his cruiser, where the reporters could not get at him and where he could not hear the less than kind things being said by the denizens of nearby Western Heights Federal Housing Project.

By the time I arrived that evening, Bob had given his statement to Tommy Stiles, a veteran homicide investigator. No one appeared surprised to see me. It is understood that an officer is not left alone after a shooting.

As Bob changed clothes in the locker room, fellow officers came by to reassure him of their support, each in his own way. "You listen here, boy," one burly cop said. "Don't you go and get upset if the newspapers ain't exactly kind tomorrow. We know you did what you had to do."

Bob Wooldridge is a transplanted Pennsylvanian from Philadelphia. Brash and loud in his calmer moments, his dark eyes flash and he grows animated as he talks. Once he drew the wrath of veteran police officers by saying at a Fraternal Order of Police benefit rally that police work is his hobby and the paycheck is just a bonus. Some thought he was serious.

At thirty, Bob has been a police officer for eight years. He never wanted to do anything else. He took his bachelor's degree in Criminal Justice at East Tennessee State University, and when the Knoxville Police Department began to hire, he jumped at the chance to live in East Tennessee.

He is witty and intelligent. Women call him "cute," with his curly hair and thick mustache. His shiftmates sometimes call him the "preppy cop" because of his stylish dress and because he ran the university beat so long.

We are an unlikely pair. Ten years older than Bob, I am not a party person. He parties frequently. He is single, while I am happily married. We are both cops, though, who have never burned out. Both of us would rather make a good arrest than eat, even when we are hungry.

We met when Bob moved into the subdivision where I was living, and we have been friends ever since. He has a key to my house, and I have a key to his. Every Fourth of July, Christmas, and Thanksgiving we get together. My eight-year-old thinks Bob is his playmate.

As we left the building that night, he turned with anguish in his eyes and said, "Damn, Hunter, I just killed a man." It was as if he had just realized it.

"Yes, you did, and I don't know how you feel. But I know what you have to remember. You did exactly what you've been trained to do, exactly what you had to do. Otherwise, you'd have been dead."

Later at home, sipping a Michelob and looking very tired, he said, "When the guy went down, I was relieved. The first thing through my mind was, *Thank you, Jesus!* I knew how close I'd come to dying. Then even before I was finished with that, I thought, *Father, forgive me, for I have sinned.* It was strange." He shook his head.

"No, it wasn't, Bob. It's just another burden for a cop to bear, one that other people will never know about. You did your job. The only way it could have been different was for you to have ignored the call. You're too good a cop for that. You did what you had to do. A sane man does not come at a police officer with a piece of angle iron."

The next day, investigators interviewed the dead man's family. He was, they said, a paranoid schizophrenic, prone to violent episodes and afraid of cops.

It was a clean shooting, what cops call "righteous." There was never a hint of wrongdoing on Wooldridge's part, either from the press or within the department. He had done what he had to do to save his life and to protect the public.

Unfortunately, it did little to ease the pain. Good police training does not erase what the Sunday school teacher taught: Thou shalt not kill. The Bible says that.

To make the act easier to swallow, police instructors have erased the word *kill* from their vocabulary. Police officers are not trained to "kill." They are trained to "neutralize the threat," to "eliminate the hostile fire," to "stop the antagonist."

Bob Wooldridge knows those euphemisms. He has heard them, but you cannot fool him. He knows what happened that night: A man tried to kill him with a piece of angle iron, and, to save his life, Bob put a projectile traveling at more than 1,300 feet per second into his chest, exploding his heart. Afterward he had to watch the man die.

He has also found out something else, a truth demonstrated by Jesus himself, when he cried out, "My God, My God, why hast thou forsaken me?" Just because you put your own body on the line to save others does not mean the pain will be any less or the scars any easier to bear.

3

Now She Sleeps in a Cab

The first time I saw her she was stark naked, strutting her stuff on a small wooden stage at a now defunct Clinton Highway bar. She was a tall woman of perhaps twenty-five, blond, with long, shapely legs. In those days she looked pretty good, though even in her best days she was plagued with a tiny pot belly. In the strip joints of Clinton Highway, however, such a minor imperfection was never noticed. The dancers never ran to beautiful. The truly beautiful girls danced in the west where the money was, and is.

Janice (I'll call her that) was not a typical stripper, at least not then. She had two small children and a husband with a steady job. She was experimenting, she told me the first night I talked to her, with "alternative lifestyles."

"Does your husband approve of this?"

"Not exactly," she laughed in a deep, throaty voice, "but he puts up with it. I make good money here."

"Well, good luck," I told her, "but it has been my experience that when you lie down with dogs, you get up with fleas. I'd suggest you go home to your children—while you can."

"No, this is fun. I'm gonna enjoy it while I can. For the first time in my life, I feel free."

She stayed on my mind for a long time that night. I hoped her husband would get a grip on the situation before the marriage went under. The Clinton Highway taverns glitter on the surface; underneath is a cesspool.

23

★ ★ ★

It was perhaps three months later when I rolled in to a domestic disturbance at Janice's house. It was in a working class subdivision, not fancy but substantial. Curious neighbors, unused to such problems, peered out their windows.

Janice, clad only in a bra and panties, was nose to nose with a big, burly man with the look of a truck driver about him. Both were red in the face as they stood in the front yard, screaming at each other. There were no signs of physical violence, but it appeared imminent.

"You're gonna stop it and come home to your kids!" he yelled as I got out of the car. I could see two small blond children peeking from a window.

"All right! Let's take this argument inside," I said.

Once in the house, the tale unfolded, as the two children cried in fear and confusion. Janice was to have been home by 1:00 A.M. because her husband was due to take a truck to Birmingham. She had not come in until 3:00, causing him to lose the load.

"I'm not gonna put up with this," he threatened.

"You agreed!" she yelled. "You promised me some freedom."

As they shouted at each other, I read the signs of cocaine use. Normally a quiet person, she was loud and abrasive. She sniffed constantly, though there were no other signs of a cold.

"Listen up," I said firmly, "this has to stop. Now!"

"That's better," I said, as the yelling stopped. "Janice, put your children to bed and try to calm them down."

While she was gone from the room, I talked to her husband. He seemed more confused than the children. Not a sophisticated man but a blue collar worker—a big man in a flannel shirt—he wrung his hands as we talked. He was in a social situation beyond his comprehension.

"I don't understand her anymore. We never had a whole lot, but we got by. All of a sudden, she wanted freedom. I thought it would pass. Now, her whole personality has changed. She hardly brings home any money. I think maybe . . ." He almost choked on the words, "she's seein' other men."

It would have been pointless to tell him how much a cocaine habit costs, both in physical and financial terms, though I had no doubt what was going on. I gently persuaded him to go somewhere else to spend the night. He left, shoulders slumping. When he was gone, I turned to Janice.

"This alternative lifestyle is about to become your only lifestyle. You better get your head together and get off the nose candy. If you don't, you're going to lose everything you've got." I moved my arm to indicate the room. There were mementos of a calmer time, pictures of the children smiling from handmade frames and elaborate needlepoint work on the walls.

"Coke's not addictive. I can quit when I feel like it," she said defiantly.

"Coke won't be the end of it," I said. "Look at the girls you dance with."

"I'll be all right," she told me with eyes downcast. "I appreciate your concern, but I don't need your help. For the first time in my life, I'm having fun."

"Officer Hunter, Officer Hunter!"

Turning, I saw Janice at the end of a line of dancers, all scantily clad and in handcuffs, waiting to be taken to jail. Warrants had been served on all of the dancers for violation of the obscenity law. Nude dancers, under the existing law, were strictly forbidden to touch customers. According to undercover officers, they had all been climbing into customers' laps, fondling, and being fondled. What they were doing was called "lap dancing."

"Officer Hunter, my kids watch television. Please take me out past the television cameras."

She appeared to have lost about twenty pounds since I had last seen her more than a year earlier. When she lifted her arm, I saw the reason why. Ugly red marks punctured the bend of her elbow. Janice was on the needle.

Waving off the television cameras, I walked her out to my cruiser and loaded her. We waited as the rest of the girls were brought out and placed in cruisers. I did not speak to her until we were on our way to jail.

"I see you've picked up a new hobby since I saw you the last time."

"Yeah." I watched in my rear-view mirror as she looked out the window. She was pale, haggard looking.

"You're not going to tell me you can quit anytime you want?" I asked.

"No. I'm hooked. We both know it. I had to ease the pain when I couldn't get enough coke."

"Are you still with your husband?"

"No. He took the kids and left. I don't blame him."

"You can still get out of this," I said. "We can get you into a program."

"I don't think so. I don't have anything to go back to."

"If you don't get out of this, you're going to end up on Magnolia Avenue." Magnolia Avenue is the end of the line. It is where addicted prostitutes walk the street.

"That'll never happen to me, Officer Hunter."

"I hope not, Janice."

She locked eyes with me in the mirror and shrugged.

Mike Upchurch waited as I pulled my file of exotic dancers from the filing cabinet. That morning a citizen had found a dead woman by the side of the road in a remote part of Knox County. Upchurch was the investigating detective.

"By the way she was dressed, I'm guessin' she was a prostitute. A lot of dancers end up in that line of work," he drawled. "She's pretty well messed up, but we might be able to identify her by pictures."

I sat down with the files, and he handed me the Polaroid pictures he had shot at the scene. Reluctantly, I looked at them, never having had a taste for blood and gore.

The woman lay, skirt bunched around her waist, one knee raised in a parody of coquettish behavior. She had died in agony, grasping grass by the handful. A close-up revealed a face that had been beaten beyond recognition. The torso and neck were perforated with stab wounds. There were slashes on one leg—all the way to the bone.

"Give me some dimensions," I said.

"Between five feet and five three, 110 to 125 pounds, mid-twenties to thirty. Hair, as you see, reddish, but maybe dyed. I didn't see any tattoos, but she was pretty dirty."

I flipped through my files of exotic dancers, eliminating those not within the ranges Upchurch had set. In the end, there were four for him to check. As it turned out, I had no file on her. We later found that Upchurch and I both knew her from our patrol days when she had danced on Clinton Highway, but neither of us recognized her because of the mangled face.

"Oh, by the way, I ran into an old acquaintance of yours on the way in. We showed the picture around on Magnolia Avenue."

"Oh yeah. Who was it?"

"That tall blond, Janice. The one that used to dance on Clinton Highway. She's about used up. She said her boyfriend threw her out because she caught the clap. She's sleeping in an old cab now."

She was sitting with her legs dangling from the back seat of the cab. Her head nodded from time to time as she stared off into the distance. I watched her for a minute, knowing that she was not aware of my presence and having trouble believing that this was the pretty, laughing woman I had first met just a few years earlier.

"Janice?" I walked around to face her. On the seat beside her was an "outfit"—a syringe, a rubber tube, a butane lighter, and a spoon for "cooking" the mix. It explained her calmness.

"Off'ser Hunner," she slurred out the words. "I thought you might be by . . . after I saw your frien'. You know, the slow talkin' detective. What can I do for ya? How about a freebie? I'm good. Everybody says that."

"You know better, Janice. I don't want anything from you. I'd like to help. I can still get you into a rehabilitation program."

"I know," she said, "you never took any of *this* . . ." She lifted her skirt obscenely and giggled, "even when I looked *good*. Why not, Off'ser Hunter?" She stared at me through bloodshot eyes. "Jus' why the hell not?"

"Because you're worth more than that. Get in my cruiser, and I'll take you to the hospital."

"I can't do it." She broke into a near-hysterical giggle. "I'm havin' fun. I'm free. Don'tcha 'member nothin'?"

For a moment I was consumed with rage. I very nearly snatched her up. I had ample reason for an arrest. It would have been pointless, though. The rehabilitation programs are full of people who wanted help.

27

"Here's my card, Janice. If you change your mind, call."

"No, if you change your mind, call me. I got a special rate for ol' frien's. Here's my card." She repeated the obscene lifting of her skirt.

Tears stung my eyes as I walked back to my cruiser. A wino sitting on the curb looked at me with a puzzled expression and held out his hand. I gave him all my change and walked on.

4

The Cop and the Outlaw

Make no mistake, he was a criminal. I have no desire for it to appear otherwise. Everything I believe about law and order, he held in contempt. There was no excuse for him, no tale of youthful poverty and deprivation. He was a criminal by choice, an outlaw who wore the name tattooed on his body.

Despite all this, I liked him.

I first saw him at a bar that features nude dancing. A fellow customer had offended him, and he had dislocated the man's jaw. I arrived in answer to the bartender's call and found him sitting calmly at a table sipping a beer. In those early days I never saw him drunk.

Nodding nervously, the bartender indicated that he was the cause of the disturbance. The injured man had been helped away by friends before I arrived.

"You have to leave," I told him.

"Why?" He took another sip of beer and wiped his mouth with the back of his hand.

"It's customary that I ask the questions."

"Is that so?"

"That's so," I replied, leaning forward, "because this is *my* highway. Now, step outside—quietly or otherwise."

His eyebrows lifted in surprise. He was not intimidated. "And if I don't step outside?"

"Then I'll drag you out."

"Are you certain you can do that?" He made no reference to the fact that he was nearly a foot taller and fifty or sixty pounds heavier than I. Dressed in jeans and an old Army fatigue jacket, he had a full beard and shaggy hair. However, unlike most outlaws, he was meticulously clean.

"Yes, I'm certain." Stepping back, I slid my baton from the metal ring. "You can go with me, or with the next five cops who come through the door. That was my last request."

"All right." He got up slowly, with no hint of embarrassment. I had no doubt that he had merely decided it was not worth the trouble. I dropped the baton back into the ring and followed him through the door.

Outside, he paused by his black Harley-Davidson motorcycle and turned. "I don't think I've seen you out here before. May I ask your name?"

"You'll be seeing me a lot from now on. This is my beat, my highway. Dodge City days are over. From here on out, you settle your differences quietly. When things get past talking, *somebody* goes to jail. My name is David Hunter."

"Fair enough," he said, hitting the starter with his foot. In those days, no self-respecting outlaw would have thought of using an electric starter. "My name's Jake. I guess you'll be seeing me a lot, Officer Hunter."

Having heard about the confrontation, another officer told me that Jake (not his real name) was a member of the Outlaw Motorcycle Club—or as they call themselves, the American Outlaw Association. Not as well known in the media as their sworn enemies, the Hells Angels, they are very similar. The birthplace of the Outlaws, however, was Chicago. They are less flashy than the Angels, the difference between the Midwest and California, perhaps. They are every bit as dangerous, however.

"Jake is a bad-ass," the veteran officer told me. "Other Outlaws clear a path when he walks in. And he's smart. Got a college education, I hear. They say he handles the cocaine trade and manages the dancers."

"I wonder what starts an educated man down that road," I asked.

"Who knows?" the other officer shrugged. "But he's definitely a man to watch if you get him angry with you."

30

★ ★ ★

"Adam 12, 10–59 in progress," the dispatcher said.

I listened carefully to the location of the "fight in progress." Being close, I jumped Adam 12's call, not waiting for other units to arrive. Still a new patrolman, I had not learned as much caution as I needed.

Striding into the sleazy little bar, I drew my baton. A tall, thin man was facing a very obese individual, menacing his opponent with a beer bottle. I stepped between them, facing the man with the bottle.

"Drop it!" I said.

A momentary expression of disbelief came over his face, then he stepped forward and swung the bottle at my head. Ducking, I drove the grip of my stick into his solar plexus, then raised up and chopped his wrist with the long end. The bottle clattered to the floor as I swung him around to put the cuffs on.

While I was snapping the handcuffs, the fat man caught me in an arm-lock from behind, cutting off my wind. I later learned that the two combatants were the best of friends who routinely beat up on each other every time they got drunk.

As I reached up to grab the arm around my neck, the fat man hissed and released his grip. Turning, I saw Jake spin the big man around and punch him once in the face. The fat man hit the floor with a grunt, where I quickly put my second pair of cuffs on him.

By the time other officers arrived to help me load the two drunks, Jake was gone. I watched for him, though, and finally spotted him a couple of nights later at an all-night diner, the type of place that sells greasy hamburgers and stale rolls.

He looked up as I slid into the seat on the other side of the booth. "You're not worried about your reputation?" he asked.

"No. Are you?"

"I guess not, Officer Hunter. I was about to have a piece of apple pie, if you'd like to join me—my treat. I do love southern food."

"Where are you from originally?"

"Ohio."

"How did you end up here?"

"There was a contract out on my life. I came down here to

31

hide for a while. The climate is great, so I stayed." It was as if a contract on his life had been a minor thing.

"I appreciate what you did the other night," I told him. "It could have gotten nasty."

He stared at me for a few moments, then took his pie from the waitress and ordered a piece for me. "You got started late in the warrioring business, didn't you?" he asked.

"I never thought of it like that, but you're right. I was thirty when I stumbled into it."

"You'll do well, if you live long enough," he said around a bite of pie. "You need to learn about watching your back."

"I guess you're right." We ate in silence for a few minutes.

"Aren't you going to ask me how an intelligent fellow like me got into the Outlaw business?" he asked, taking a sip of coffee.

"I didn't think you'd answer."

"Probably wouldn't have if you'd asked. Since you didn't, though, I'll tell you. I'm an Outlaw because I was born out of time. This is a dull century, Hunter, a very dull century. It's a time that traps a man's soul. The things we own weigh us down. The only thing worth having is what you can take with you."

"And what might that be?" I asked.

"A code of honor."

"You don't have to be an outlaw to live by a code of honor. I live by a code of honor."

"Yeah, but you've got a mortgage, a car payment, and kids to support. I own my scooter and the clothes I'm wearing. A real Outlaw can't love anything but the code. Everything else weighs him down." He got up and picked up both tickets.

"Do all Outlaws get so philosophical?" I asked.

"Naw, most of them are a bunch of dumb-asses." He smiled for the first time. "Just like most of your buddies."

Over the next year or so, I would nod to Jake as we passed each other in bars or other places. He drank a little, but was always in control. Then he violated his own code.

Jake fell madly in love.

She was a pretty thing. A natural blonde, nineteen or so, who claimed her father was a police officer in another state.

She moved in with Jake, and thereafter he was always around when she was working. He began to neglect outlaw business.

As Jake watched her dance naked each night, he grew depressed. In the outlaw world a woman is an object, not a person. They dance nude, turn tricks, and give all the money to their "Old Man." To show jealousy when she left with a high-roller with a pocket full of money would have been *total* disgrace. Two things outlaws are not allowed: intravenous drugs and to be in love.

He was rip-roaring drunk, sitting behind the wheel of an old Pontiac he had just driven into a ditch, when I arrested him. I helped him from under the wheel. He blearily looked at me, staggering to the back of the car.

"I offered to take her away from this, Hunter. I offered to retire from the club. She likes it, though. She likes sleeping with strange men. That makes her a whore, doesn' it?" His words were slurred.

"I don't know, Jake. I'm not a priest; I'm just a cop. You're under arrest for drunk driving."

"Can't you take me home? I don't usually drive drunk. You know that. Give me a break."

"No . . . ," I hesitated. "I have to do it."

"You're right. It's in your code. I unnerstan' that. I really do."

It was the first of many arrests for drunk driving. In a few months the club had sold his motorcycle to pay off his debts. He caught four months in jail for his third drunk driving charge. While he was there, his "old lady" took his car and moved to Florida.

I transferred off patrol, and it was a year before I saw him again.

"This sounds strange, officer, but I've been appointed to represent a biker," the puzzled lawyer said over the telephone. "He asked me to call and tell you that he doesn't have any cigarettes or money. I have no idea what he wants."

"Would that be Jake?" I asked.

"Yes. How do you know him?"

"I used to put him in jail. Thanks for calling."

33

While I was at lunch, I bought a couple of packs of his brand of cigarettes. That afternoon I went down to the jail and had him brought to an interrogation room. He had thinned down some and looked pale in his orange jumpsuit, Knox County jail issue.

"What's the charge, Jake?" I pushed the cigarettes across the table.

"Conspiracy to distribute cocaine. The Feds got me." He opened a pack and lit up.

"You back in the club?"

"No. Trying to get back in. I was repaying some debts. I got in bad shape for a while. That woman almost did me in, Hunter. I was crazy about her."

"Jake, it's a sad thing when the only person you can turn to is a cop who used to put you in jail."

"I know. It's my own fault, though."

"Why don't you deal? You know enough to get into the witness program. You can walk a free man, Jake."

"I can't turn on the brothers, Hunter. You know that." He shook his head tiredly.

"They sold your motorcycle. They won't even bring you a pack of cigarettes, for God's sake! You don't owe them anything!"

"I owe myself," he said. "You can understand that. It's a matter of honor. I lost it for a while, but I've got it back now."

"No, I don't understand. If you change your mind, though, I'll help you get to the right people." I stood up and shook his hand.

"Hunter," he said as I was leaving, "watch your back."

5

Black Friday
Coming Down

April 1, 1988, was Good Friday, the day when Christians commemorate the crucifixion of Christ. The officers of the Knox County Sheriff's Department, however, were not able to fully appreciate the religious significance of the day. Before it had ended, they were calling it "Black Friday." It was at the center of a seven-day period that left sheriff's deputies wondering what would happen next.

The previous Tuesday, Gary Williams, a veteran officer assigned to Baker shift, had been patrolling his beat in South Knoxville when a car crossed the median and crashed into his cruiser. The cruiser was heavily damaged, and Williams was sent to the hospital with head injuries.

A police supervisor is not as fortunate as a football coach: there are no substitutes to send into the game. Captain Bill Wilson, the Baker shift supervisor, was short a patrol officer until Williams could return. Night shift, from 10:00 P.M. to 6:00 A.M., is not a good time to be short of patrol officers.

Police calls in Knox County generally begin to pick up on Thursday evening. The action peaks Saturday night and Sunday morning, then begins to drop off again.

It was just after midnight Friday when Baker shift patrolman Larry Moore and his partner for the night, reserve officer Steve Webb, were dispatched on a bank alarm coming from a mobile home being used as a temporary branch building.

Moore, a veteran cop known for his impeccable courtesy, was not too excited. Bank burglaries in this day of sophisticated alarm systems and near impregnable safes are rare. There was a breakdown in the system that night, however. Looking through the window, the two officers were surprised to see a man with stacks of money in front of him on the floor.

"I couldn't believe it," Larry told me later. "He was nonchalantly stacking up money. This guy wasn't even a professional, just a transient who happened to be in the right place to commit a crime of opportunity."

Spotting the officers as they spotted him, the suspect dived out a window and fled. The officers quickly followed in foot pursuit, with Webb slightly in the lead.

Hitting a fence on the run, the suspect attempted to go over it. When Steve Webb grabbed him, he turned and stabbed Webb in the hand with a screwdriver, breaking loose.

Minutes later, with officers still in close pursuit, the suspect attempted to commandeer a vehicle at a nearby market and service station as the owner was pumping gas. The suspect jumped into the car and started the engine.

Officer Moore grabbed the suspect and attempted to drag him out. The suspect pulled away, dragging the determined Moore along the pavement.

A woman passenger in the front seat opened the door and jumped from the vehicle. But another woman in the rear grabbed the suspect by the hair, distracting him and allowing Officer Moore to regain his feet as the vehicle slowed.

Reserve Officer Webb entered through the open passenger door, and the two officers were able to pull the struggling suspect out of the car and cuff him. He was charged with, among other things, aggravated assault, burglary, and attempted kidnaping.

When the adrenaline stops flowing, the pain sets in. While not seriously injured, both officers were battered and bruised and were transported to a nearby hospital.

Later in the morning, at six o'clock, Adam shift hit the streets to relieve the weary Baker units. As officers generally do at that hour of the morning, most of them went in search of hot, black coffee.

On the way out, a BOLO (be on the lookout) was broadcast. Three prisoners had escaped from nearby Meigs County that morning, two men and a woman. The suspects were thought to be in a stolen Chevrolet Cavalier.

Minutes later, officer George Ogle, a big man with a shaved bald scalp, thought he had seen the Cavalier at a motel just off Interstate 40. Broadcasting his information, he went back but could not locate it again.

Coffee was forgotten. Officers Denny Scalf and Larry Hunter converged on the area to assist Ogle. Minutes later, the vehicle was spotted in the drive-in lane of a fast food restaurant. Fearing that the suspects might have firearms, Hunter cautioned the other officers to wait until the car had left the restaurant.

As the Cavalier pulled back onto the road, the officers boxed it in. Abruptly the vehicle turned onto the lot of a truckstop. Whipping in and out among the parked rigs, blue lights flashing, the officers pursued. At the back of the lot, the suspects drove into an open field.

Familiar with the ground, Officer Hunter knew the vehicle would bog down in moments. Jumping from his cruiser, he started across the field on foot. Almost immediately, the vehicle floundered in a ditch, and the suspects abandoned it.

Hurtling across the field in waist high grass, Officer Hunter suddenly found himself approaching a wide ditch. Seeing that he would not be able to stop in time, he attempted to jump across, but did not quite make it.

When a man trained with firearms begins to fall, there is one central thought. *Where is my weapon pointed?* The gun hand must be protected at all costs. As he crashed into the embankment on the other side, all his 195 pounds impacted on his left wrist, dislocating the elbow joint and chipping the bone.

As it appeared that the suspects were about to escape, George Ogle took aim and fired one round. The round missed, but two of the suspects went down in surrender. The third was tackled by a civilian who had been watching the action from nearby.

Shortly, with the suspects all recaptured, Officer Hunter was being treated at the same emergency room where Moore and Webb had been earlier. Three officers had gone down in a seven-hour period.

Meanwhile, I was sleeping soundly. It was my birthday, and I was scheduled off, intending to relax all day. My wife, Cheryl, woke me up.

"Larry's been involved in some kind of incident with murder suspects in the west end. They've taken him to the hospital. The radio didn't give any details."

Instantly awake, hands shaking, I grabbed my radio and called the field supervisor. Lieutenant Joe Brooks, an old friend and classmate, told me that everything was all right. An hour later, I walked into the emergency room.

"The other half of the 'Brothers Grim' has arrived," someone joked. Someone had tagged the nickname on us after Larry followed me into police work. Both of us are noted for our aggressive style.

The emergency room was full of cops wisecracking, making jokes, and telling obscene stories, as they always do when shaken up. The emergency room personnel ignored the breach of etiquette; cops are well liked there. They knew it had been a rough night.

After my brother had surgery to set his arm, the doctor told me he would be able to work again, but the prognosis for full recovery was not good. He was right. The pain never quite went away, and the elbow has never regained its flexibility.

It was 4:00 A.M., April 4, when Mike Upchurch woke me. "I wanted to tell you before you heard it on the radio. Mike Loveday crashed over on Broadway a couple of hours ago."

It was the third Baker shift injury in a week. Upchurch had called me because I was a former member of the "Killer Bees," a shift noted for a high level of arrests and aggressive work. I had helped train many of them and had been trained by others.

"How is he?" It was a silly question. Mike would not call me at 4:00 A.M. unless it was serious.

"Doesn't look good. I wanted you to be ready—just in case." He let it hang there.

"What's wrong?" Cheryl asked, as I hung up the phone.

"Mike Loveday has crashed. It doesn't look good." There was nothing more to say. Such calls had been fairly frequent in my years with the department. We try never to let an officer hear bad news over the radio or television—not when one of his friends is involved.

The next day I pieced together the story. Around 2:00 A.M., Loveday had driven up on a black Mustang doing "doughnuts" in the road. Spotting Loveday, the driver fled, turning off his headlights. The officer radioed the dispatcher that he was going into the city after the vehicle. It was Loveday's last transmission that morning.

Minutes later, patrolman Ed Cummings, on his way to assist, told the dispatcher why Loveday was not answering her.

"Baker 16 has wrecked," Cummings said.

Loveday had apparently lost control on the wet street, and the new Plymouth cruiser had struck a power pole, the rear end hitting first. The car looked like an accordion. The rear of the vehicle ended at the front door, and Loveday was trapped between the protective screen and the steering wheel. It is thought that the spare tire from the trunk struck him in the back of the head. Gasoline covered the pavement; the blue lights were still flashing. They could not be turned off until rescue people raised the hood and cut the battery cables.

As Loveday was being removed from the car, the Knoxville City Police and Officer Cummings found the suspect in the black Mustang. He was no fleeing felon. He had run because he did not want to be arrested for traffic violations. A cop had suffered near fatal injuries so that a traffic offender would not have to spend a few hours in jail.

The odds did not appear to be in Loveday's favor. He was in critical condition, in a coma. However, at twenty-eight he was strong. Although there was no response for days, his wife put a radio beside the bed. We assured her that a good cop would hear his radio no matter what.

Intensive care personnel were frantic as they tried to keep cops away, but they kept coming, believing that Loveday would hear them if they talked to him enough. Finally, by April 12, he regained consciousness. The doctors said it was just short of miraculous.

He was moved to the Patricia Neal Center for therapy, and I did not see him for a few weeks, not until Joe Shelton's funeral. Joe, a veteran officer, had been killed in an automobile accident while off duty.

Standing by the door, badge draped in black mourning ribbon and wearing white gloves, I was directing guests to the proper room when I saw Mike come in on his wife's arm. He had lost weight and was moving slowly, but he was on his feet.

He stood for a moment, not speaking, then embraced me. I hugged him too, not caring who was watching or what they thought. So what if cops do not cry in public? So what if cops do not embrace? My brother was back from the edge of death's kingdom. Battered and weak though he was, he was back.

At some point between Black Friday and Shelton's funeral, I went to a small restaurant frequented by cops, just outside the city limits. I nodded at the two city detectives who were already there and found a table at the back.

I had just taken a seat, when I saw the elderly woman rise and start toward me. *Here it comes,* I thought, *complaint number 380. "Why aren't your people out enforcing the law, instead of hanging around restaurants?"*

"You work for the sheriff's department, don't you?"

"Yes," I said gruffly.

"How are the officers who were injured at the first of the month?"

"Better than we thought they would be, ma'am."

"That's good." She was a tiny woman with wispy white hair and pale skin that looked like fine porcelain. "I know people don't tell you very often, but I wanted you to know that we appreciate everything you do for us. I pray for you every night before I go to bed."

"Thank you," I managed to choke out, staring down at the table.

People were looking at me as she walked away. I was ashamed and suddenly not very hungry. I got up and left the restaurant, sitting in the car for a while to compose myself.

I was glad the elderly woman was praying for us. There was no doubt in my mind that her words carried weight with God.

Cops sometimes need divine intervention. Especially when we have days like Black Friday coming down.

6

"I Was a Legend"

"**D**isturbance in progress," the dispatcher said. "Subject refuses to pay his bill or leave the motel. The clerk advises that she has been threatened."

Heading toward the motel, I sighed a deep, self-pitying sigh. For two days I had been suffering from some variety of influenza. Weak and tired, I was working because I knew somebody else would have to pull my load if I was not there.

The motel, just off Interstate 75, had more than its share of problems. Because of low room rates, not only travelers, but locals, made it their temporary home. The clerk, a pretty, freckled girl in her early twenties, was frightened, but also furious.

"I've called him several times since check-out time. The last time he stormed in here, threatening me with violence. He's drunk, which is the way I've seen him every time he stays. I want him out of here!"

"I'll talk to him, but if he refuses to come out, there's not much I can do. Until you file charges, it's a civil matter."

"You'd better get a backup before you go over there," said Jason, the man who acted as maintenance and security. "That guy is mean, real mean. I don't know what his problem is, but he's got a grudge against the world."

"All right, I will." Expecting no real problems, I nonetheless called for a backup unit. In my weakened condition, I did not need to be involved in a brawl. Drunks generally will not

41

come outside a door, knowing that they become immediate fair game for arrest once they do.

"It's that room right there," Jason said, as we arrived.

Rapping on the door with my PR–24 baton, I waited. Moments later, the door was snatched open. An angry man was on the other side, his hair silver gray, almost white. He was in his fifties, faced creased like parchment. About six feet tall, his weight approached two hundred pounds.

"Whatta you want?" He blew alcohol-saturated breath in my face.

"I'm Officer Hunter. I have a complaint that you caused a disturbance in the front office."

"I didn't call you, and I don't need you!" He started to close the door, but I held it with my toe.

"Why don't you just pay your bill and leave? That way the management won't sign warrants and have you arrested."

He stepped from the room and, like an overgrown child on a playground, began bumping me with his chest. "Why don't *you* just get in your little cruiser and drive away. Tell the sheriff's department not to send a boy to do a man's job the next time."

"You're under arrest," I said, "for public drunkenness."

His pale, watery eyes squinted for a moment, as if it had just dawned on him that he had left the sanctuary of his room. With a sneer, he turned as if to reenter it.

"Don't try to go back in the room. You're under arrest," I told him.

"Try and stop me!" He whirled and took another step as I caught him by the shoulder and spun him back around. He went berserk, dropping his head and hitting me with his shoulder.

Sidestepping and slipping out of his line of attack, I realized how weak I was and wondered how far away my backup was. Snarling, he turned once more to attack. I raised my PR–24 and blocked his assault, causing him to sting his hands and forearms.

"Stop it!" I yelled. "Or I'm going to hurt you!"

He came at me again. This time I punched with the handle of my baton, striking him just above the solar plexus. I knew it had to hurt. With desperation in his eyes, he tried to run past me into the room. Fearing that he might have a weapon there, I charged in and hit him with my shoulder, knocking him away.

Gasping for breath, with rage in his eyes, he turned to face me again. I cocked the PR–24, preparing to put a "spin" on it. Properly used, this baton will take the wind out of a big, big man.

"Stop it and get on the wall. I'm through playing. Do it, or I'm going to send you to the hospital!"

Reluctantly he put his hands on the wall. Reaching for my cuffs, I slid the baton into its holder. As soon as the baton dropped, he tried to come off the wall. Silently we struggled. I had one hand behind him and managed to close the cuff.

"Give me a hand," I yelled at Jason. Moments later, I had his hands cuffed behind him. He did not stop fighting, though. All the way to the car he cursed, kicked, and threatened.

My backup unit arrived as we rounded the building. We managed to stuff the suspect in the car, though he was still kicking and clawing like an alley cat.

"Real tush-hog," my backup said.

"Yeah," I replied, getting out my notepad to record the name and address of the clerk who had called. The information turned out to be unneeded, though. She was killed in an automobile accident before the case came to trial.

"You think you're really something, don't you?" the man snarled as we pulled away. "Think you're really bad. I know your kind. You're sleepin' with the little desk clerk back there, playin' hero. I know how it works. I used to be a cop!"

"What did they fire you for?" I asked.

"Bastard!" He kicked at the back of the seat. "I used to eat punks like you for breakfast. You're a punk!"

"I arrested you, didn't I?" Debating with drunks is pointless. I knew it, but I was upset and my neck was already tightening. I would still be at the emergency room having x-rays made when he got out of jail. I was laid up for several days with muscle strain.

"You needed help, though! You couldn't do it by yourself!"

"That's nonsense," I answered, "and if you were ever really a cop, you know it's nonsense. I just didn't want to hurt a drunk old man. I could've ended it the second it started."

"You bastard!" he roared. "I was a legend out here when you were in diapers!"

"Maybe you were," I shrugged. "Now you're just an old alky, fighting with the cops. I've arrested a hundred just like you."

He was still cursing and insulting me when we arrived at the jail. Ignoring him, I pulled his criminal history. He was on probation for assaulting an officer, and he had several public drunkenness and disorderly conducts. I charged him with public drunkenness, assault and battery on an officer, and resisting arrest. It was over a year before the case came up. I was not at all worried, considering the case to be open and shut.

"It *looks* pretty open and shut, but you never know with this lawyer," the assistant attorney general told me.

"You mean they're actually asking for a trial, with *his* criminal history?"

"Just remember, we can't introduce his criminal history unless he opens the door by bringing it up. Maybe we can't use it then. This judge doesn't believe in it. He wants each case tried on its own merits."

"I've got faith in the jury," I said. "They'll see right through him."

I was wrong, though.

Jason, the part-time security guard, did not do well as a witness. The defense attorney made him look like a crafty publican, hounding and harassing innocent guests. Our star witness, of course, was dead.

"Officer Hunter, would you describe this alleged assault on you. You say in the warrant that he 'bumped' you. Explain it."

I went over the scene, describing it as best I could. I realized that the lawyer was trying to make it look as if I had overreacted, making it appear to have been a boyish confrontation.

"In other words, it was similar to something that might happen on a playground between children?"

"Yes, sir, if one of the children weighed two hundred pounds and was bumping a police officer."

The lawyer shrugged, looking at the jury with a knowing look, as if to say, Wasn't this a lot of excitement about nothing?

The jury, of course, had no way to know how terrified the

desk clerk had been or that the man had a long history of violence and drunkenness.

At last the defendant took the stand. Neatly dressed and sober, under the skilled questioning of his lawyer, he proceeded to tell the jury that he was a retired police officer. It was hinted, but never said, that he was a lonely man living from one motel room to another.

He told the jury that he had consumed a few drinks in the privacy of his room, having no problems until the hotel security called him before checkout time to curse and threaten him. He then told the jury that the security man opened his door and let me in. He said that I viciously attacked him with a nightstick as he lay in bed.

Further, he told them that after I dragged him off to jail for no reason, the hotel staff stole several hundred dollars from his room, hinting that I shared in the profit.

Under cross examination, he was asked why he had not reported the alleged missing money or the supposed brutal beating delivered as he lay innocently in bed.

Almost weeping, he told the jury that he was so hurt that a police officer with my training and experience would do such a thing to a brother officer that he could not bring himself to talk about it to anyone. He was the most accomplished liar I have ever listened to.

At one point he slipped up and mentioned a former arrest. The assistant attorney general jumped at the opportunity, but the judge, who was also the judge who had placed him on probation for his last assault conviction, refused to allow the prosecutor to pursue the questioning. He said the case would be tried on its own merits.

When the jury went out, I was still confident. It had been established that I never knew the man prior to the incident. I am an officer, known to be a man of integrity, and I testify well.

The shock was unbelievable when the jury acquitted him on all charges. The man looked at me with an ugly expression of triumph. It was the first case I had ever suffered an acquittal on. The jurors would not look at me.

"Do they think I just made this up?" I asked the prosecutor.

"No, I don't think so. He was just so credible, he raised

doubt. Also, he's nearly sixty years old. That brings in sympathy."

I was devastated. I had always had faith in the jury system and its ability to get at the truth. It seemed impossible that someone had assaulted me and walked away.

Later, I heard from one of the jurors, who approached me in the lobby of the City-County Building.

"Officer, I just wanted you to know that we didn't think you were lying."

Without speaking, I stared at the elderly woman who had helped turn a dangerous man loose. She went on hurriedly.

"He was getting old and had served honorably as a policeman. We felt sorry for him. It seemed he had too much to drink and made a mistake, and he seemed convinced that he believed what he was saying. We didn't think that anyone is that skillful a liar."

I still did not reply. It was pointless to rehash the matter, and I would never convince her anyway. "Well, I wanted you to know. We believed you were doing your job, but we decided if there was any doubt, we didn't want to put someone his age in jail."

Nodding at her, I went on my way. It was a good lesson, though. Never again would I look at any case as open and shut.

The bad guys hire skillful lawyers, and the last thing on lawyers' minds is what *really* happened.

7

My Home Is My Castle

Tennessee law once allowed a man to discipline his wife with a stick, so long as the stick was no bigger around than his little finger. The size of the stick was established by court decision.

That particular law, of course, passed away long ago, but the reasoning behind it hung around until 1986. It was reasoned that a man's home is his castle and should be free from interference from the state. Following this path of logic, anyone who lives in a man's castle is subject to his discipline. No allowance was made for the women subjects residing in the castle.

Mind you, the law did not come out and say it's all right to whip your wife as long as you do it in the privacy of your home. There was no need to say it. It was understood.

This logic has followed its own peculiar path in every state. In Tennessee it had its roots in the distinction between a misdemeanor and a felony. A felony in Tennessee is any crime punishable by imprisonment for a year or more in a penitentiary. A misdemeanor is any crime punishable by a year or less confinement, generally in a county jail or similar place.

An officer can make an arrest on a felony in Tennessee, based on probable cause. This can be defined as "information or evidence that would lead a reasonable person to believe that a felony has been, or is about to be, committed." Because of the less serious nature of a misdemeanor, Tennessee legislators, in a legitimate attempt to curtail "warrantless arrests," said that a misdemeanor *must* be witnessed by an officer before he can make an arrest on the spot.

In theory, this is a good idea. In practice, it makes an officer's job very difficult. Nowhere was the problem more glaring than in domestic disputes. Simple assault, which can be defined as "an assault made without a weapon, and with no obvious intent to maim or kill," is a misdemeanor in Tennessee, as are such public order crimes as disturbing the peace and public drunkenness.

That legal reality frustrated police work beyond words. An illustration is the best way to explain. We will call the family the Todds and the road where they lived Ogle Road. The Todd house was an address well known to all officers who worked that end of the county.

"Baker 10, domestic dispute in progress, Ogle Road. The complainant says Mrs. Todd is crouched beside the road, one block from her residence."

"Ten–four," I replied. The dispatcher did not have to tell me where the Todd residence was. I had been there many times, always with the same result.

A few minutes later, I was cruising along Ogle Road looking for the victim. Suddenly she darted out in front of the car, holding her arms across her enormous breasts, barely covering herself. She was clad only in a pair of sheer panties. An overweight redhead, the forty years or so of hard living were well written on her pale face.

"He's at it again, I see." I opened the door for her, then walked back to the trunk for a blanket to cover her.

"Yes," she said, shivering despite the warm weather.

"Why don't you leave, Mrs. Todd? You have a job. There's no reason to endure this kind of abuse."

"Why won't the neighbors help me when he does this?" she began to sob. "Because they're afraid of him, and so am I. Everything I have in the world is tied up in that house, and I have to think about what would happen to my children if he kills me!"

"Do you think it helps your children to see this?" I asked, knowing the futility of it all. We had been through it before.

"It only happens once in a while."

"At least sign a warrant for assault and battery, so I can

48

arrest him tomorrow. Let us throw him in jail, and he'll stop doing this to you!"

"He'd kill me when he got out. You can't hold him but a little while before he makes bond. Just take me up there and let me get some clothes, then I'll go to my oldest daughter's house."

"I was there a week ago, Mrs. Todd. Your oldest daughter's husband beats her pretty regularly now. I wonder if she puts up with it because she saw you do it?"

"Just let me get my clothes," she said, dropping her head.

"All right. We'll go up there, but you know what's going to happen." I knew what would happen, and I was already boiling with rage just thinking about it.

I pulled the cruiser up in front of the small, neat frame house. Walking up on the porch, I tapped on the door with my baton. In a moment, Todd opened the door. He was a big man—six feet tall and about 240 pounds—with thinning blond hair. His belly flowed over his belt in waves.

"What the hell do you want?" He looked over his shoulder. I saw that two of his friends were sitting at the table, a card game in progress. A fifth of Jack Daniel's was in the middle of the table.

"Your wife needs some clothes. She's going to your daughter's house."

"Tell her to buy some clothes. She's got money, and she sure don't spend it on anything I want. I can't even get her to buy a case of beer once in a while." He started to close the door, but I put my foot in it. He looked at me, eyes flashing like a spoiled child.

"You'd better get your foot outta my way, or I'll file a complaint. I know the law, and I know my rights!"

"One of these days," I said quietly, shaking inside with rage and frustration, "you're going to make a mistake and step outside that house. When you do, you belong to me."

"Get the hell out of here." He laughed, looking back at his friends who also smiled at my discomfort. "You can't arrest a man for being drunk inside his own house." I moved my foot, and he slammed the door.

"Please sign a warrant, Mrs. Todd. Tomorrow is my day off, but if you'll sign it, I'll come back and arrest him."

"I can't do that," she said refusing to look at me. I drove her to her daughter's house.

The frustration of having to walk away from battered women turned some police officers into con artists. I backed another officer up on a domestic violence call one night shift. (He has asked me not to use his name so he can keep his "official" image intact.) We arrived at a decrepit trailer, with rust running down the sides.

Beside the trailer, however, was a shiny new boat and a Harley-Davidson motorcycle, which was worth more than the trailer and the lot it was on.

"We ain't got no problems here," the man who answered the door said. He was of medium build, shirtless, with several tattoos on his body. Behind him a frail woman with stringy hair sat on a couch. The front of her dress was stained with blood, and she was holding a wash cloth with ice in it on the bridge of her nose.

"Well," the officer said casually, smiling a big country boy smile, "one of your neighbors complained. I can see everything's all right, but we need to come in. You know, just so the boss won't accuse me of loafin'." The officer sounded casual, but I knew him well. I had seen the tightening of his jaw muscles when he saw the woman with the bleeding nose.

"All right," the man said with a sneer, "but I know my rights. You're comin' in only because *I* say so." The man swayed drunkenly. There was a strong odor of alcohol on his breath.

"Sure," the officer said. "After all, it *is* your home."

"Damn right it is," the man said, slurring his words.

"Are you all right, ma'am?" the officer asked.

She nodded her head affirmatively. We both saw that there was also a bruise on her left eyelid.

"Sure, she's all right. She's got no complaints," the man said, picking up a can of Coors.

"Why don't you go wash up, ma'am, so we can talk to your husband." She immediately got up and walked back through the trailer. It was obvious that she was used to following instructions.

"Women," the officer said, shaking his head, "you have to

whack 'em into line every once in a while, or they'll try to run your life."

"Hell, yes," the man said, belching loudly. "They think they own you. You guys want a beer?" He stumbled to the refrigerator and got another Coors, then giggled. "I guess you can't drink on duty."

"Yeah, a woman's mind just doesn't work like a man's," the officer said. "Every time I spend a little money on my Harley, the old lady gets bent out of shape."

"You ride a Harley?" the man slurred, popping the top on the beer.

"Yeah, 'course I don't have a beauty like that one outside, but I hope to some day."

"I got ten thousand in that baby," the man bragged, taking a swig.

"Some day when you're not busy, I'll drive by and you can show it to me," the officer said, standing as if to leave.

"Hell, I'll show you *now*." He bent over and pulled on his work boots. "Hit that switch by the door. The flood lights are on it."

I looked at my brother officer as we all went out the door, but he did not bat an eye. "Lock the door behind you," he said quietly to me.

"I started with a '57 frame," the man said, waving his arms enthusiastically, "then I . . ."

"I don't care anything about that piece of junk. You are in a public place in an intoxicated condition. I am placing you under arrest for public drunkenness."

"You can't make me come out, then arrest me! I know my rights."

"This officer can testify that you walked out voluntarily. Stagger over there and put your hands on that first cruiser."

The man made a clumsy dash for the front porch. I stood, blocking his way, but my brother officer caught him by the arm and hair before he got to me and spun him back out into the grass.

"Keep it up," the officer said. "I can really get down, if you want. I don't think so, though. You'd rather pound on a ninety-pound woman. So get over there and assume the position, King Kong. I'm sure you know it well enough by now."

When I left, he was patiently explaining to the man what would happen if his wife were ever found in such a condition again. The officer was also explaining that a good officer *never* forgets a car, a motorcycle, or a face.

To my knowledge, there was never a call there again. Street cops have always known what the "experts" have just discovered. Men who abuse women do not like sitting in jail, even for short periods.

I had one further encounter with Mr. Todd before ending my patrol career. Tennessee's new domestic violence law went into effect July 1, 1986, putting domestic violence under "probable cause." It was still early July when I went back.

My heart jumped with joy as I headed that way. Another unit responding to the call caused me to pick up speed. I feared he would arrive before I did.

We met each other at the driveway and sprinted for the door, passing Mrs. Todd who was standing at the mail box clad only in a bathrobe. The side of her face was swollen. Mr. Todd leaned against the door frame with a beer in his hand, seeming to enjoy himself immensely.

I have seen ferocious dogs turn and run when confronted with a person who shows no fear of them. This is the best analogy I can think of for what happened next. The sneer on his face began to vanish as I crossed the yard at a run, followed by another eager cop. As my foot hit the first step of the front porch, his eyes widened and he attempted to slam the door.

I hit the door with my hand before it could snap shut. "Cover the back door," I yelled over my shoulder. The big man got to the hallway before my hand closed around his thick leather belt. I braced myself, bringing him to a halt, then swung him back toward the door. He stopped and raised his fists as if to fight, a look of desperation in his watery eyes.

It was the smile, I think, spreading over my face as he raised his arms that made him reconsider. He dropped his arms in dejection. "You can't come into a man's house like this," he sniveled.

"You are a very big disappointment to me, Mr. Todd. You outweigh me by sixty pounds, and you do so enjoy beating up on smaller people. What's the problem?"

"You got a gun," he said.

"Well, I'm just glad you've already justified your cowardly behavior. Turn around and put your hands behind your back."

The other officer came through the door at that moment. "Congratulations," he said, "I've been waiting for this opportunity since the week I started runnin' out here."

"Maybe you'll get the next one. There are still plenty out there. We'll never be back here again, though, will we, Mr. Todd? The next officer through that door might not have the same respect for civil rights that I do."

He began to weep softly as I led him handcuffed, shirtless, and barefoot across the yard. His wife stood—mouth open—and watched. Neighbors came out on the porch and buzzed among themselves as the mighty ogre who had terrorized a neighborhood was loaded into a cruiser by a man who barely came above his shoulder.

"It's against the law to come into a man's house without a warrant," he said in a quiet voice.

"To the contrary, Mr. Todd. It is now illegal for me *not* to take you to jail if there has been any violence, or even if your wife says she's afraid. Do I make myself perfectly clear? We now have a domestic violence law. Every time you decide to slap your wife around, one of us will be here to throw your sniveling carcass into jail. You do understand that, don't you?"

"Yeah, I understand." He did understand, too. I ran into his wife at a shopping center a few months later. She looked like a new person. I asked her how things were going.

"Very well," she smiled. "He'll probably never be a nice person, but every time he raises his hand, I remind him of the police car. He's never hit me again."

Police work does have its little compensations.

The most horrible of all domestic violence situations, though, is one where the woman has convinced herself that there is no hope. In such cases a woman has no self-esteem and somehow sees herself as responsible for the abuse. The domestic violence law cannot help this woman. Even when the solution is at hand, she will not accept it.

I rolled into a trailer park on a domestic violence call one warm fall evening, followed by another officer. It was a nor- .

mally quiet park, consisting not only of permanently anchored trailers but also numerous smaller trailers belonging to people on the move. It was a pretty, wooded area.

The woman was standing under a tree near one of the smaller trailers. At first I thought she was a child. Upon approaching, however, I saw that she was a petite woman about thirty years old. She was fragile, about five feet tall, maybe eighty pounds. Her skin was the color of lightly creamed coffee, with the features of an American Indian. Her hair was straight and raven black, falling to her waist, and her eyes sparkled like polished onyx. There was a bruise on her left cheek bone, and her dark skin was streaked with tears.

"Did you call for an officer, ma'am?"

"Yes, I appreciate your coming so promptly." The accent was soft, southern, maybe from middle North Carolina.

"What seems to be the problem?"

"There's really no problem. I came out here to tell you that everything is all right now."

"It looks like you have a bruise on your cheek. Would you like to tell me about it?" Sometimes frightened people need a little coaxing.

"No, it's all right. We had an argument, but it was my fault."

"Most arguments don't cause bruises. I'm David Hunter. What's your name?"

"Ruby," she said, "Ruby Banks. I caused the problem. I know better." She did not offer to go back inside. Through the front door I could see a large man, apparently asleep on the couch.

"What did you do to cause this, Ruby?"

"I took a bus into town to see a movie. I was late getting back and didn't have his dinner ready."

"Does he always put bruises on you if dinner is late?"

"No, just when he's drinking."

"Well, Ruby, around here we call that assault and battery. It's against the law."

"It's nothing," she said. "Two years ago he did this." She took my hand and placed it on her right outer thigh. There was a large knot.

"How did he do it?" I glanced at the other officer who was standing quietly nearby.

54

"He knocked me down and jumped up and down on my leg until it popped," she said. "He was sorry about it, though, when he sobered up."

"Where did this happen, Ruby?"

"Over in North Carolina. That's where I met him. I was working in a nuclear power plant there. He's an engineer, a consultant on turbines. Right now he works for the Tennessee Valley Authority."

"Did you notify the police about what he did?"

"Yeah, but they said as long as I was married to him, there was nothing they could do. I know that's the way it is. I know your hands are tied, but I appreciate the fact that you came when I called."

"Well, Ruby, it just so happens that we have a domestic violence law in this state. All you have to do is tell us you're afraid of him and invite us into your home. We'll take him straight to jail."

"I have to sign a warrant, right?"

"No. I'll sign a warrant for domestic violence, by assault and battery. Just say the word."

She stared at me, as if the conversation had taken an unexpected turn. "I didn't know that."

"Well, it's true. Are you afraid? Shall we remove him?" The bruise was growing darker. I sincerely hoped she would ask us to take him, because I wanted to help her and because I wanted the pleasure of snapping the cuffs on him.

"No . . . I can't." She dropped her head.

"Why not?" the officer beside me asked.

"I don't have anywhere to go, or any way to get there if I had a place."

"You have a car and a jeep by the trailer. Surely you can write a check or use a credit card," I said.

"No, I can't. He buys straight shift cars so I can't drive them. We have credit cards, but they're all in his name. I still wouldn't have any place to go. I don't have a family, and after twelve years I don't even have any friends." I couldn't believe she had been enduring this treatment for twelve years.

"If there was a place where you could go without money and people would give you a fresh start, would you go?" I asked. I was becoming involved on an emotional level. All the textbooks say you should never do that. A cop with no feelings, though, is not fit to be a cop.

"I guess I would." She was looking down again.

"Well, it just so happens I can take you to a place like that. It's a shelter for battered women. They'll provide you with a lawyer and help you get your share of the property. He won't even know where you are."

Her black eyes locked with mine. For a moment I saw a woman with a glimpse of hope in her eyes. Then she shook her head.

"No, I'd have to leave the kitten," she said softly.

"What about a kitten?" I asked.

"Once, when we were over near Charlotte, I ran away from a beating. I had a little puppy I'd found. When I came home, he had stomped it to death."

I looked through the door at the man on the couch. He had turned over on his back and was snoring, mouth wide open. At work he was a professional, probably looked up to by fellow workers. There was probably no indication that he jumped up and down on small women and puppies when he was drunk.

"Excuse us just a moment, Ruby." I huddled with the other officer a moment. We debated a course of action. We knew the situation, but the woman had not invited us in or asked for help. We agreed that one or the other was necessary to protect us from a false arrest suit.

"Ruby, I'll take your kitten to a safe place—to my house, if I have to. Let us take you to a shelter, or let us take him to jail."

"No," she lowered her head, "I know you're really concerned and I appreciate it. Everything I have in the world is in that little trailer, though."

"Ruby," I said gently, "nothing in that trailer is yours. Sometimes it's best just to start over."

"No." Her voice was almost a whisper. "I just can't do it."

"Ruby, I want you to tell me where you met him so I can go over there and *buy* a woman just like you." I saw the look of shock on my fellow officer's face as I said the harsh words. I was making a last ditch attempt to get her out, even if it was not in keeping with departmental public relations policy.

Her head snapped up, and there was fire in her eyes for a

moment. "Don't you belittle me! I was a nuclear power plant operator once. Do you know what's involved in learning that?"

"Yes, Ruby, I do. I wasn't smart enough to even get into the program when I tried. You can do anything you want. You don't have to live like this. Get your kitten and some clothes. Let us take you to a shelter."

She looked at me and smiled for the first time. It was not a happy smile, though, but bittersweet.

"You're a nice man. I know what you're trying to do, but I can't. I really can't." She pointed with her chin to the trailer. "He's nice most of the time, and he *needs* me. I just have to try harder to please him."

We stood quietly for a few moments. I knew there would be no happy ending here. From my pocket I pulled out a card and handed it to her.

"Ruby, on this card is a list of your rights under the domestic violence law. We've explained them already. On the back is a number for the shelter if you change your mind."

"Thanks," she said, then turned and walked away. I watched her go back to the trailer and her kitten. There was a slight limp from the deformity on her thigh.

For the rest of the shift I was in turmoil, unable to leave the call behind as the police manuals say you must. I thought of my own daughters and the heritage I am leaving them.

The next evening I drove by and the little trailer was gone. Perhaps she told him, when he sobered up again, what had happened. Maybe they moved on to where the law still does not protect women.

I can hope, though. I hope she got out. I hope her confidence was restored and that she has children and puppies galore.

Good luck, Ruby.

8

That Old Time Religion

The first time I saw him, he was walking, head down, the picture of repentance. Under his arm was a Bible given to him by the religious study group that had been instrumental in his "conversion." His words were soft as he answered the judge's questions.

It was hard for me to believe at the time (I was a "new buddy," a green jailer) that this soft-spoken "gentleman" was charged with a brutal rape and execution-style murder. I found it easier to believe once I saw how he was able to terrorize a cellblock full of hardened criminals, ranging from rapists to armed robbers. He reigned supreme, a shark in a tank full of barracuda.

To the outside world—to the religious community that ministered in the jail—he was a changed man, a born-again Christian. He would sob softly as they prayed with him and an hour later would be exacting painful revenge from a cellmate who had somehow angered him.

Fortunately, the jurors who heard his case were not among those who wanted to give him another chance. They saw with their own eyes what he had done and how he had done it, and then sentenced him to die, deciding to let God sort it out. His advocates are still working on getting him a second chance, however.

There are as many Bibles in a jail as there are decks of cards. I do not devalue religion or those who go down to the jails with sincerity in their hearts. I have seen the power of true conversions. They are all the more miraculous to me because I have seen the bogus conversions, put on as easily as most of us put on a coat.

A letter from a minister carries weight when a judge is making a decision about sentencing or when the classification process is going on at the penitentiary. It pays to have religion in jail. Jailers who know all about inmates have no input in the decision. If you want truth about an inmate, ask a jailer or the officer who deals with him on the streets.

A few years ago, I answered a disturbance call in a racially mixed neighborhood. A black family was involved in a domestic dispute that had spilled out into the front yard. As I approached, I saw that a crowd of white youths had gathered two houses down to watch. One of the whites, who looked familiar, yelled out, "The niggers causin' the problem are over there!"

Pulling up, I got out of the car and walked among the disputants. They quickly separated on command and listened with downcast eyes as I explained why they would have to settle down and go back inside.

The matron and supreme head of the family thanked me. She is a big, beaming woman of warm ebony color who raised numerous children and now is working on a house full of grandchildren. "I appreciate that you handled this without arrestin' anybody. They good boys, offisuh. Just git a little rowdy sometimes."

"I know, Mrs. Wilt. You've raised them to respect the law and other people. Just tell them to hold it down."

Mrs. Wilt was an old acquaintance. One wet winter evening years earlier, I had been in the field behind her house searching for a lost child in the bone-chilling cold. As I passed behind her little frame house, she came out with a pot of hot coffee and homemade doughnuts.

"It's the way I was raised, Offisuh Hunter. More than I can say for some people around here."

The crowd of whites was still in the front yard. The word *nigger* could be heard above the laughter and catcalls being directed up the road. It was being spoken intentionally loudly so as to be certain that the Wilts heard it.

"See you later, Mrs. Wilt." I had enough problems, without

a racial incident that day. As I cruised back down the road, I looked closely at the crowd. Upon examination of the man who had first yelled at me, I saw why he looked familiar. He was a regular at the Knox County jail, a petty thief.

"Come here, Austin," I said, not bothering to get out of my cruiser.

"Yeah? How come you didn't put them niggers in jail? They always put me in jail for causin' problems."

"Come close, Austin. I don't want anyone else to hear this," I told him.

He leaned down in a conspiratorial manner, looking back as if to show his friends how important a man he really was. He was a scrawny, unwashed looking individual.

"Austin, do you know that lady up the road? Mrs. Wilt?"

"Yeah, I know her."

"So do I. You're not fit to sweep her front walk. If I hear the word *nigger* come out of your mouth again or if I catch you out here causing any more problems, I'll throw your ass in the Knox County jail for disturbing the peace!"

"You listen to me . . ." his face went scarlet.

"No, Austin. *You* listen, because I don't take static from loud-mouthed thieves. You've got thirty seconds to get inside. If you open your mouth again, you ride. Now move!"

Of course, he complained. The captain talked to me the next night. "He says you came out there and humiliated him in front of his entire Sunday school class. Furthermore, he says he hasn't been in jail for over three months, and he doesn't like for you to insinuate that he's not an upstanding Christian. The chief says to remind you that we talk to everyone the same, convicts or preachers."

"He may *be* a preacher pretty soon," Upchurch drawled. "A bunch of ex-cons have started a church, and he's a member."

"I could tell by the way he was talking to his neighbors last night that he's just bubbling over with the milk of human kindness and brotherly love," I said.

"You're a cynic, Hunter," Upchurch said. "That man has seen the light—or figured out some way to make money off of religion. I hope they don't make him the treasurer."

The church struggled along, building a little at a time. We

61

watched with interest. It was the only church around where the members did not wave as we drove by.

Then we were called there one Saturday in answer to a burglary. Someone had stolen two new air conditioners.

"I don't understand it," the pastor said. "Who would do a thing like this? What kind of person would steal from a church?"

Upchurch bit his tongue until the preacher went back inside, shaking his head. "I wonder," Mike asked, "if the members of the Board of Deacons can account for their whereabouts last night?"

The church is still there, though many of the early members went back to their former professions of rape, looting, and pillaging. I recently read a report, though, that made me understand that they have not yielded entirely to orthodox religion.

The present pastor had come in to file a complaint. A certain young man, it seemed, had asked to be considered for the office of deacon. After much soul searching, the elders had determined that he was not a "mature" enough Christian.

When informed, the would-be deacon promptly punched out the pastor and had to be thrown out of the church bodily. He resented being told that he did not meet the criteria of a deacon, as outlined by the Apostle Paul.

Religion is a controversial subject. I myself sometimes attend Pentecostal, Episcopal, Baptist, Methodist, and Unitarian churches.

Orthodoxy eludes me. My religion is personal, not worn on my sleeve. My more traditional friends say that I am not tolerant enough. They may be right. They say I should not make judgments about the sincerity of others. They tell me that God will judge and give everyone what they have coming.

At the risk of being judgmental, though, I will say this. When the trumpet sounds and we are all called to judgment, I would rather be sitting with an honest agnostic than with a two-faced hypocrite who has used the name of God for his own purposes. I believe there will be less danger of stray thunderbolts.

9

"Somebody, Please Look at Me"

I was about to start the car, steaming coffee and a small pack of chocolate doughnuts on the seat beside me. It had been a slow night, the kind that makes cops more weary than working hard. "Officer Hunter, could you wait just a minute?"

She was one of the clerks from the store, with a worried expression on her face. She inclined her head towards an old Toyota by the gas pumps. A small man with long, curly hair was walking away from it.

"What is it?" I asked.

"Would you stay around for a few minutes? That guy has been in here several times lately. We think he's crazy or on drugs. He waits until we're by ourselves, then walks around making threats and calling us names."

"All right. I'll stay close by." An officer receives a lot of similar complaints. Looking relieved, she went back inside.

I pulled over into a vacant lot next to the all-night market, opened my doughnuts, and took the lid off my coffee. In a few minutes, the man came out and walked back toward his car. He tensed as he spotted me, then tried to act casual as he pumped his gas.

As he pumped the gas, I looked at him in more detail. He was small, about five feet, six or seven, maybe 130 pounds.

His hair hung in curly ringlets to his shoulders, and he was dressed in what I would call a "tough guy" costume: ragged blue jeans, boots, and a sleeveless tee shirt.

When he seemed to become more jittery with each passing second, casting glances in my direction furtively, my suspicions were immediately aroused. Cops make everyone nervous, but not to that degree. There was something wrong, some reason he did not want my attention.

Nearly twenty minutes were spent pumping what I later learned was one dollar's worth of gas. Finally he put up the nozzle, then cleaned his windshield. He opened the car door and bent over as if he were looking for something.

Without warning, he jumped into the old car, fired up the engine, and screeched away, apparently thinking he would get away before I could move. The air was filled with the scream of the engine, which either had no muffler or a defective one. There were no lights at all on the rear of the car.

Before, I had only suspicion, no reason even to speak to him. The lack of a muffler, the screeching tires, and the missing taillights gave me all the reason I needed to stop him. I wheeled out behind him and hit the blue lights. When he made no effort to stop, I bumped the siren.

Without warning, he turned left across the four-lane highway toward a road that headed to the next county a short distance away. It would make no difference, though. I had witnessed a violation in Knox County and under hot pursuit policy could follow him to Canada. Most civilians, though, operate under the assumption that officers cannot leave their jurisdiction.

It became a moot point as his engine died, and the old Toyota coasted to a stop on the shoulder of the road. I stepped from the cruiser, weapon drawn but held by my side. He jumped from the car, panic in his eyes.

"I wasn't tryin' to run!"

"Hold it right there! Get your hands out to your side where I can see both of them. Walk to me slowly. Stand in front of my car."

"I wasn't tryin' to run, really!" His behavior was erratic, verging on panic.

"I didn't say you were trying to run, did I? Raise your arms and turn all the way around once." At close range I could see that he had no place to conceal a weapon under his tight clothing.

"If you weren't going to run, why didn't you stop as soon as I hit the blue lights?"

"I didn't know you meant me," he said. "Honest to God."

Cops know that when you hear the name of Deity invoked, you have either just heard a lie or are about to hear one. "Give me a break. Don't insult my intelligence."

"All right! I panicked. Is it a crime to panic?" The rage leaked through his eyes.

"No, but it is a crime to flee from an officer. I need to see an operator's license."

"It's in the car."

"All right," I said, becoming more alert. Suspects often lull an officer, then grab a weapon from the front seat. This man was definitely not behaving normally. He acted as if he were on some type of speed, although I smelled the odor of an alcoholic beverage. He should have been heavy lidded and drowsy.

"I'll follow you to your car. Don't reach in until I put my light in there. No sudden moves at all. Understand?"

He reached gingerly into the front seat. I had holstered my weapon, but my hand was on the butt. Turning, he tried to hand me the wallet.

"You hold on to it," I said. "Walk back to where you were." I was standing in mud up to the top of my shoes. His car had coasted into a place where water was standing on the shoulder.

Brian Merritt, the patrol officer assigned to the beat, had come to check on me. Seeing that everything was all right, he stopped and threw his light into the passenger area of the suspect's car.

"Do you know why I stopped you?" It was strange that he had not asked. It is usually the first indignant question.

"I figured the women back at the store had lied about me or something."

"Why would you think that? Have you had problems with the women at the store?"

"No, but I couldn't think of any other thing I might've done." He would not look me in the eye.

"What kind of lies do you think they might have told?"

"Well, they might have said I called them names or somethin' . . ." His voice trailed off.

"You said you hadn't had any trouble with them. Why would they say something like that about you?"

"They acted like they were better than me! *That's* why!" The rage slipped through once more.

"I stopped you for having a loud muffler and no taillights," I said.

"Oh," his face lit up. "I shoulda had them fixed. That's for sure."

"You've been stopped before, haven't you, for the same thing? This car sticks out like a sore thumb."

"Yeah, I guess I have."

"Did you get a citation? Were you drinking when the last officer stopped you?"

"I'm not drinkin' now, honest to God."

"Don't shuck and jive me, son! I'm a street cop. I *smell* it on you."

"All right, I had two beers earlier, but I'm not drunk." The rage and defiance were close to the surface, but he was controlling it pretty well.

"I didn't say you were. I did ask, though, if you got a citation for the taillights and muffler."

"No, I didn't get a ticket. They gave me a break."

"*They!*" I raised my eyebrows.

"Two or three, I don't remember," he said. "I've only had the car a little while."

"You have a lot of luck. Is there any reason why you didn't get a ticket from any of those officers?"

"Well," he tried a boyish grin but did not quite carry it off. "My dad is a cop, so they let me off with a warning." He acted as if the matter were settled, and he was relieved to have it over with.

It was the answer I had expected.

"Look," Brian Merritt said from the suspect's car. He was holding a set of nunachucks, a karate weapon consisting of two short sticks held together with a chain or rope. "They were on the floorboard on the driver's side."

"I can explain them," the young man said, swallowing hard.

"Explain them to Officer Merritt, while I check you for warrants and valid license."

"Well?" Merritt asked, standing in the headlights of the car.

66

"I've got these juveniles chasing me, all right? I bought the 'chucks for protection. A man's allowed to protect himself. Right?"

"Nobody has the right to carry unauthorized weapons in this state," Merritt said. "When I find them, I always wonder if they might end up being used on me one night."

A stocky man, a competent cop with eyes nearly always on the verge of smiling, and an eight-year veteran of the department, Merritt knows all about weapons. One night on a dark road in west Knox County, he caught several slugs in the chest. Fortunately, his body armor stopped them. He does, indeed, understand weapons, the darkness, and caution.

"It's not like I've got a gun or a knife," the young man said defensively.

"It's *exactly* the same as far as the law's concerned, but I'm not going to charge you," I answered. "I *am* going to write you a receipt and confiscate the weapon, though."

For a moment it appeared that he was about to protest, then he saw me with the citation book in my hand. A look of disbelief passed over his face.

"You're writing me a ticket?"

"Yes, I am. I think two or three warnings should be sufficient for anyone. Also, I think when a man gets to be twenty-one, like you have, it's time to stop using your father's name. Sign here. It's not an admission of guilt, just agreement to appear for court."

His hands were shaking as he signed the ticket. At the time, I thought it was relief. Later I would realize that he was barely controlling the rage boiling in him. I did not know at the time that I had tipped a precarious balance somewhere in his personality.

"All right," I said, "Officer Merritt has given you a receipt for the unauthorized weapon, and I have given you your citation. Your car is not safe to drive. Would you like to go to a phone and call someone to come after you?"

He nodded assent, not looking me in the eye as I opened the back door of my cruiser. Merritt and I pulled out at the same time. He continued down the highway, while I stopped at the all-night market a block away.

"Something else," I said as I let him out of the car. "You

obviously have a problem with the women who work here. I can't tell you to stay away, but I would strongly suggest it."

"All right." He went into the store and used the telephone, not looking in the direction of the two employees. When I left after speaking to one of the clerks, he was standing by the road, waiting for his ride.

My shift had ended at three in the morning. I had barely fallen asleep when the phone rang around four-thirty.

"Officer Hunter," the dispatcher said, "a suspect you wrote a ticket to earlier has filed a complaint against you. You need to meet Unit 503 at his office."

I went to the kitchen to keep from disturbing my wife and called the homicide officer to a meeting channel. At Knox County, homicide division handles all major crimes against persons.

"Carl, can't this wait until tomorrow? I just got to bed a few minutes ago."

"Negative. I need you and Brian in my office as soon as you can get here."

"Ten–four," I said tiredly. A complaint was nothing new. Being called in by the homicide unit was.

"What's wrong?" Cheryl asked sleepily.

"I've been accused of something. I have to go in and be questioned by Carl Seider."

"Do we need to call a lawyer?" She looked alarmed. Cops' wives are pessimistic.

"No. I haven't done anything wrong. I haven't even been involved in anything that could be construed as wrong. The only thing I did tonight was write a ticket. Don't worry about it. I'll be home before you leave for work." I hoped I would anyway.

Merritt had already arrived when I got there. Like me, he tried to appear casual, but a knot had appeared at the bottom of his jaw.

"I want to turn state's witness," I said. "Tell me what Merritt did, and I'll sink him." The laughter broke the tension. Inside the office, it returned.

"I'll have to Mirandize you," Carl Seider said awkwardly, the way you always do when a cop is on the other side of an investigation. A tall, thin man, Seider looks like a scholar and is. He holds a Master's degree in Criminal Justice from the University of Tennessee. He is a thorough investigator. Despite a long friendship, I knew he would put the nails in my coffin if the evidence told him I was guilty. He knows I would do the same to him, no matter how painful.

Carl took my statement, stopping me from time to time to interject a question. When it was over, he turned off the recorder. "This young man has accused you and Merritt of aggravated assault. I took his statement at the hospital."

He held up a picture of the man with his back to the camera. I flinched at the row after row of welts across his back, not because they were particularly severe but because I realized how much pain he had endured in an attempt to destroy two officers he had never met before I stopped him.

"Looks like he was beaten with a belt or cord, something flexible," I said.

"He alleges that you made him assume the position on the car and that Merritt knocked him down with a set of nunachucks, then handed them to you. He says you beat him across the back as he lay on the ground, then alleges that you returned with your nightstick and beat him some more. He says that after beating him, you drove him to a telephone. Tell Brian to come in."

Discussing the case with Carl would not have been proper, but I felt better. Even involved as I was, I could see the obvious flaws in the story. First of all, the stripes on his back had not been caused by a blunt object. The injuries would have been much more extensive. Second, the stripes were almost geometric and went around the curve of his body. To receive such injuries, he had to be standing in one position the entire time. He had obviously been beaten with a flexible object.

When I saw, on the way out, that Carl had dusted my car for prints to determine if the man had been placed in position to be searched, I realized exactly how thorough he intended to be.

While I was at home worrying all day Wednesday, the man showed up at the internal affairs office to file a complaint. He was agitated. Rather than filing a complaint, however, he wanted to discuss his relationship with his father and how he had never been able to live up to a "macho" image.

Lieutenant Bob Greene continuously steered the conversation back to the issue, but the young man wanted to ventilate about his father and his own problems. When the lieutenant asked if he would take a polygraph, at first he agreed. Upon finding that he would have to take it that afternoon, he walked out of the office without ever having made an official complaint.

Meanwhile, Seider found that the man's own witness did not support his statement. He had told Seider that his friend had picked him up and had taken him to the hospital. There was a time gap. He had not mentioned the alleged beating to his friend until he called a second time. Further, Seider found no prints or smears on my car, where it was alleged that I had placed him.

The phone rang in the early morning hours the following Friday. I had worked the day shift as usual on Thursday. It was Mike Upchurch. Working an extra job, he had been monitoring the radio.

"That guy who accused you of beating him is back on the highway. He has a rifle or shotgun, and Charlie Shift has him surrounded. I thought you'd want to listen in."

I turned on the radio and listened. I heard officers, obviously under great strain, talking back and forth. By the sounds of their voices, I could tell that tension was heavy. By listening to voice tones as well as words, I knew they were on the verge of shooting the young man, who was stalking back and forth with a weapon in his hands.

He was demanding by turns that his father be brought to the scene or that Merritt and I come out so we could "settle our differences once and for all." They were unable to locate his father. Merritt had called in sick that night, and I was home in bed.

Finally, I heard a relieved Charlie shift officer report that he was in custody. The weapon was an air rifle. I went back to bed thinking of what might have happened had I been working. It was a chilling thought.

The young man had apparently realized that his ploy was not working. So during the early morning hours, he had stormed into the all-night market and told them that Merritt and I had beaten him once again. He demanded that we be called to the scene, then left the store.

A short while later, officer Dave Gaddy saw him in a parking lot about a block away. When Dave pulled in, the young man stepped from the car with the weapon in his hands. Gaddy immediately called for back-up and a homicide investigator. Had the responding officers been less experienced or less steady, the incident would have ended tragically.

"I can tell you one thing," Gaddy later told me. "He was out there prepared to die, and he wanted his daddy to see him. He was walking back and forth. It was like he was saying, 'Look at me!' He wanted attention, and he was prepared to die for it."

I was uncomfortable for a long time afterwards. Had the young man come at me with a weapon in his hands that night, there is little doubt what would have happened. I already knew he wanted to destroy me. The same would have applied to Merritt.

I probably will never know what pushed him over the edge. Maybe I reminded him of his father. Maybe it had been coming anyway, and I was just the catalyst. Whatever the reason, he went off the deep end that night. From jail, he was sent for treatment at the state psychiatric hospital.

I once read that the worst thing that can happen to an ordinary man is to have an extraordinary father. When I look at my son, I try to remember that he is his own person and that I must not set standards which conflict with what he is. It is a chilling thought.

10

The Legend of Bobby and June

Most Americans, secure in their belief that the great welfare state can fix anything, believe that all "learning impaired" individuals can be found in serene environments, smiling and weaving potholders, laughing like happy children.

There are two glaring fallacies in that view. Most learning impaired people do not live in sheltered environments; they fall through the cracks in the system. Furthermore, they are no nicer than their more intellectually gifted kinsmen.

Two such people are well known to the police and jailers in Knox County. We will call them Bobby and June Steel. Cops always think of them together, even though Bobby once had another wife. He is a few years older than she, but it seems that they have always been around. They're almost always together, at least when neither of them is locked up.

Bobby has no patience with people who use phrases like *learning impaired*. Once, after arresting him, I reminded him that he had been arrested numerous times for the same types of offenses and asked him if he was ever going to learn any better.

"I'm retarded, Hunter. Nobody expects me to learn. That's why I never stay in jail very long." It was, I decided, a very astute observation and absolutely true. Bobby has been arrested countless times beginning prior to his adolescence. Thieving is the only trade he knows, except for his ability to con "regular" people.

Both Bobby and June draw Social Security checks, both being considered totally disabled. Living as a unit, they also draw a welfare check, food stamps, and other benefits; and they live almost rent free in government subsidized housing, lacking for nothing. For recreation and extra money, Bobby is a burglar and June is a shoplifter.

The first time I met them was while I was working as a jailer in my early days with the sheriff's department. Bobby "went off," which is cop talk for losing one's temper or going berserk. Both of them were incarcerated at that time—Bobby for receiving and concealing, June for shoplifting. June was going through one of her regular pregnancies and Bobby, being the doting father that he is, insisted on seeing her. As there are regular visiting times, he was refused.

I was called from the backwalk to help subdue him. A big man, weighing maybe 250 pounds, with hair generally cut to the scalp, Bobby is a handful when off the deep end. Five or six of us made our way with him from his cell to the front holding area as he screamed at the top of his voice, "I wanna see my June! I wanna see my June, now!"

He could, of course, have been subdued instantly had we been allowed to handle violent prisoners as they need to be handled. Finally, several tired and battered officers cuffed him to the bars. All the while he was yelling at the top of his lungs, "I want my June, now!"

We had just gotten him under control, when the matron ran out to tell us that June also had "gone off" and had attempted to start a fire in her cell. Word travels mysteriously inside a jail.

An inmate who threatens or attempts arson immediately finds the cell stripped to bare metal. Nothing combustible is left. Minutes later, three officers were restraining June to the best of their ability, while two of us were tossing her belongings into the hall. June weighs almost as much as Bobby and can hold her own with him in a brawl.

She was screaming at the top of her lungs, "I'm a pregnant woman, and I want my Bobby, now!" From time to time she would get her arm loose and slam one of us in the back as we worked.

A stack of letters, neatly tied with a ribbon, hit the floor in the walkway. June suddenly broke loose, requiring a fourth officer to join the fray.

"Love letters," she screamed. "I want Bobby's love letters back!"

The other women inmates had gathered at the end of the walkway to watch the action.

"You don't need Bobby's love letters," one of the women yelled. "You can't even read."

"That doesn't matter," the sergeant said, struggling with June. "Bobby can't write either."

We almost lost control of the gargantuan woman as we were all seized by a fit of giggling. It was true. They are both totally illiterate. The "love letters," we discovered, were all blank.

It was some time later when I personally heard from the duo again. Off duty, I stopped to visit with Bob Wooldridge, a friend of mine who is an officer with the Knoxville Police Department. He was washing his car when I pulled up.

"Hunter, do you know a June Steel?" he asked as soon as I was in range.

"Yeah, I know her, and her husband." A big smile crossed my face. I knew the story was going to be interesting.

"Well, I met her and her husband yesterday. I got a disturbance call and when I pulled in, June was at one end of the house out front with a claw hammer. Her husband was at the other end with a big stick. They were waiting on the mailman to bring the Social Security check. Both of them wanted it. God, they must weigh five hundred pounds between the two of them!

"I told them to go inside or go to jail. They argued, but finally went in. The husband must have intercepted the mailman, because I got another call.

"When I got there, she was in the middle of the front room with a claw hammer. She had wrecked the place. I told her to drop it, but she just kept screaming."

With my smile growing broader, I settled in to listen. I knew where it was going.

"She's big, but a woman. I charged her and grabbed the

hammer. Hunter, that bitch picked me up, bounced me all over the room, then *threw me through the damned wall!*

I was laughing loudly. "I'm just glad they're on your beat, not mine."

"That ain't all, Hunter. After we got her calmed down, I asked her why she did what she did. She told me that I was trying to take her hammer and that it was the only heirloom her grandmother left her."

A few weeks later my words came back to haunt me. I fell in behind a pickup truck with no tags. There also were no taillight lens or bumper, and wires and metal dragged the ground. I hit the blue lights, wondering who would be stupid enough to drive such a junker on the road.

"What's goin' on, Officer Hunter?" Bobby's big round face, with the usual week's growth of beard, beamed at me from the cab of the truck.

"Bobby, when did you get out?" You always asked him *that*.

"Three days ago. Me and June got a trailer over on the highway. People at the church down here are helpin' us." A new church was good for a month of handouts, or until the duo staged a pitched battle during services or were caught stealing from their benefactors.

"Bobby, you've got a half dozen violations on this truck. Do you have a license and registration?"

"Sure I got a license." He immediately handed me an expired learner's permit. It was stamped: Failed Test.

"Bobby," I said with a sigh, "you have to pass the test, not just *take* it. Do you have registration for the truck?"

"No, I just give him the money, and he give me the truck." At that moment I noticed the speakers on the floorboard, four of them. They were clearly marked with the names of two drive-in movie theaters.

"Bobby, where did you get the speakers?"

"Uh, uh, uh . . ." His brow furrowed with an effort for a quick answer. "They was in the truck when I got it!" He smiled at his quick thinking.

"Bobby, they're not hooked up. Where did you get them?"

"Everybody does it, Hunter. I needed speakers for this here new truck. Me and June just went to the movies and got 'em! Nobody's gonna miss a couple of 'em."

"Get out of the truck, Bobby. You're under arrest." I bowed to the inevitable.

"*For what?*" His square jaw came out. I was about to call for back-up when Mike Upchurch rolled in behind me. Fighting with a berserk 250-pound Bobby is not pleasant.

"For driving without a license, violation of the registration law, and larceny—if the theaters want to prosecute."

He came out belligerently, then seeing Mike Upchurch with the nightstick in his hand, submitted to a patdown and cuffing. "If this is how you're gonna treat me, I ain't stayin' on your beat, Hunter!" The theater managers would not prosecute, so he was out almost immediately.

He did not leave my beat, as he had threatened. The loss of his vehicle only caused him to commit burglaries closer to home. I was off duty when the next event occurred.

A rookie, unfamiliar with Bobby found him limping down the road at 2:00 A.M. The story was later related to me, something like this.

"You need a ride?" the officer asked.

"Nope." Bobby hobbled on, trying to appear nonchalant.

"What are you doing out at 2:00 A.M.?"

"Just gettin' a little exercise."

"What's wrong with your leg?"

"Broke it yesterday," Bobby replied, increasing his hobbling gait.

"Just a minute," the officer said. Bobby immediately tried to run but went down flat on his face. It is hard to run efficiently with a three-foot crowbar down your pants leg.

Two nearby buildings had been broken into, but he had found nothing of interest. It was, after all, just a hobby for him. He was charged with burglary and possession of a burglary tool. Once again, everyone involved decided that prosecution was more trouble than it was worth.

Driving in his neighborhood one afternoon, I saw that he had finally made good his promise to move, but he had not traveled far. He had moved from the northwest part of the county to the northeast side, still in my jurisdiction. It was the week before Christmas when he turned up again.

"I pulled up," the complainant said, "and saw the old red car in front of my house. There was a guy behind the wheel. I thought it was funny that someone would be parked there. Then the front door opened, and this great big guy with a belly over his belt came out the door carrying all my Christmas presents. I yelled, and he started running. He couldn't see over the big stack of presents, though. When he got to the embankment, he just ran right out into the air and dropped about ten feet. The packages flew everywhere. The guy in the car got out and helped him up."

Bobby had dropped all the presents. Later we would find that he was teaching his younger brother the trade.

During that same period, I heard on the radio a civil warrants officer who had gone to their apartment to take custody of their newest baby.

"Get me some help over here," the officer said. "Bobby just ripped up the warrant and threw it on the floor."

For years, Bobby and June regularly had children, and the authorities regularly took them by court order. I understand that one judge attempted to have them both sterilized, but civil libertarians said it would be a violation of their civil rights. They went on being fruitful for years, until nature ended it.

The last time I saw Bobby, I had stopped by the jail and there he was, being booked. He was home, renewing old acquaintances. He greeted me like a long lost friend, and I chatted with him for a while.

"How's June?" I finally asked, after the usual pleasantries.

"She was in the hospital, but she's better now."

"What was wrong with her, Bobby?"

"We had a test tube baby," he told me.

I stood looking at him for a moment. I was certain that no doctor on earth would deliberately reproduce Bobby and June, but I was puzzled as to where he got the concept in the first place. Then I realized what he meant.

"You mean that June had a tubule pregnancy?"

"Yeah, and almost bled to death," he said emphatically.

I have been away from patrol for a while, so I seldom see the pair. They are still out there, though, living off the fat of the land and working at their hobbies.

It is not what most of us would call a fairy tale romance, but it has endured longer than a lot of "normal" marriages. They are comfortable and happy with each other.

11

Where the Wheel Fell off the Wagon

Police officers across the United States are much alike. They have similar problems, whether they are in California or New York. However, each region has problems that are found nowhere else.

Since 1980, I have chosen to be a cop in East Tennessee. When I sit down with an officer from Illinois or Utah, we understand each other, although there are cultural differences that are only learned by experience.

"East Tennessee," our more prosperous neighbors used to say, "is where the wheel fell off the wagon. The pioneers were too lazy to fix it, so they stayed. Why else would anyone have chosen to live there?"

On the surface, they seem to have a point. East Tennessee is all up and down. Early settlers could not grow any crop here on a really large scale. It would have been pointless anyway. There was no way to transport anything out of the area effectively. The rivers were not navigable year-round, and roads were little more than trails.

The early settlers grew vegetable gardens on hillside patches to feed themselves. The cash crops were tobacco and corn. Tobacco could be moved in profitable quantities; the corn went out as whiskey.

Had they but traveled west for a few more days, the pioneers could have had the rolling hills of Middle Tennessee or the fertile flatlands in the western part of the state. Instead, they settled in a place where you cannot see much more than a quarter of a mile in any direction. East Tennessee is all hills, valleys, and mountains. You are either climbing up or going down.

The French passed through, but few stayed. It was the Scots, for the most part, who took up residence. I have never been to Scotland, but I have talked to those who have. They tell me that East Tennessee is enough like the highlands of Scotland to bring tears to Scottish eyes. There are still annual Highlander festivals held each year in the region.

East Tennessee, of course, was already inhabited, not by one, but by two ethnic groups: the Cherokee Indians and a little known people who had been contemptuously called Melungeons by the French, who first encountered them. The word meant "mongrel" because the French mistakenly thought them to be a mixture of the white and Indian races.

The "civilized" English, who established the first permanent white settlements, had trouble coping with the Cherokee culture, particularly the custom of the blood feud. Simply put, it meant: You hurt or kill one of mine, and I'll hurt or kill one of yours. Any member of the other clan would do.

The Scots, on the other hand, had no problem understanding this. It made sense to them. The blood feud has never really vanished from the culture of East Tennessee.

It was not the wealthy and contented Scots who came here, for such people never leave home. My ancestors, the Hunters, had sworn allegiance to the Nixons back in Scotland; here they swore allegiance to no man. They settled among the McDonalds, the Cummings, and the Campbells. They left Scotland as Presbyterians but founded the Primitive Baptist Church somewhere along the way. Today these "Hard Shell" Baptists are more Calvinistic than any Presbyterian alive.

The Melungeons, the other ethnic group already here when the French first arrived was so intent upon privacy that they made everyone else seem outgoing. A dark people, with raven hair and eyes that ran the gamut from black to pale gray to blue, they had such names as Goin, Collins, and Mullins. Except in Claiborne County, where they became politically powerful, they kept to themselves, even refusing to take part in the political process.

This suited the canny European people. In 1834, the Tennessee state legislature declared that the Melungeons were a "colored race" and as such could not vote, own property, sue in a court of law, or marry a white person. Their neighbors simply moved in and took their land by force, the law reenforcing their actions.

Most of the Melungeons retreated to a place called Newman's Ridge in Hancock County. During the Civil War, they carried out raids against both the Union and Confederate forces. Today you will find many of their descendants still there, still a shy, retiring people.

My mother was a Goin, descended from the Melungeons of Claiborne County. There they *were* the political power. Fearing their neighbors, they called themselves "Black Dutch," denying their heritage. It was successful. It was only after I stumbled across the literature during a research project that I discovered that my mother was a Melungeon.

Knox County, Tennessee—my home—is situated on the Tennessee River and is often called the "Gateway to the Smokies." From any high point you can see the mountains.

In Knoxville, you will find the main campus of the University of Tennessee, theaters, art galleries, and libraries, in short, the culture and amenities you expect to find in any other progressive southern city.

Within a thirty-minute drive, however, you can find the descendants of the early settlers living much like their ancestors of 150 years ago. Like most inhabitants of the region, I was unaware of this until it was brought home to me a few years ago when I was dispatched to a hospital to investigate a shooting.

Ordinarily a homicide officer would have been sent. There was some doubt, though, as to jurisdiction in the shooting. "Just check it out," the dispatcher said. "If you need an investigator, I'll send one."

At the emergency room I met with the resident physician. He was wearing a pair of gold-rimmed glasses, which he removed to massage the bridge of his nose. He looked tired.

"Are you here about the gunshot victim?"

"Yeah, what's the story?"

"I hope you can find out. She won't tell us anything, not even her name. The ambulance picked her up on Interstate 40 after a passer-by saw that she was bleeding and called in. The ambulance driver thinks an old red pickup truck followed him in, but he couldn't be sure."

"What kind of wound?" I asked.

"That's the funny part," he put his glasses back on. "I took a piece of double ought shot out of her back and three pellets of number five out of her left arm. The pellet in her back was bleeding pretty freely, but turned out to be minor. The number five pellets were lodged just under the skin. Whoever dropped her on the interstate probably thought it was worse than it was."

"Sounds like she got caught in a crossfire," I said. "Can I talk to her?"

"Sure. Matter of fact, I can release her as soon as we get our information."

I found the woman lying on a stretcher in one of the trauma rooms. Her pale blue eyes focused on me, then darted away as I entered. On the chair next to her was a faded cotton dress, plastic sandals, and a raggedy bra and panties. Her age was hard to place. She was a young forty or an old thirty.

"Ma'am, I'm Officer Hunter of the Knox County Sheriff's Department. I need to ask you some questions."

"I never ast fer no lawman to come in here. The shootin' wuz a accident, it wuz. I don't need no lawman. Never have, 'n never will." It was obvious that she would have preferred to deal with the devil himself than talk to me.

"That may well be," I said, "but the State of Tennessee wants to know about shootings."

"I said it wuz a accident. Got nothin' else ta say about it. Even if it weren't a accident, it ain't air way to call in the law. We take keer of air own problems."

"Let me put it another way. You can't leave until I get the information I need. You may not like it, but it's the law." I hoped the bluff would work.

"Oh, all right. I wuz a'squirrel huntin' with my man Burl. He farred at a bushytail 'n a ball bounced back and hit me. 'Ats the whole story."

I decided not to confront her with the fact that you do not

82

hunt squirrel with double ought buckshot or that she had been hit with two different types of shot. Curiosity was beginning to get the better of me. I was fascinated with her accent. I had not heard it since my grandmother died.

"What's your name?" I asked.

"Mary Campbell." She pronounced the last name as Camp-bell.

"How old are you?"

"I was borned in 1950. May one."

"What's your address?"

"Do you know whar Johnson's Nob is?"

"No, but your mailing address will be fine."

"Ain't got nary mailin' address. Don't git mail."

"What's the name of the place where you live?"

"Johnson's Nob," she said promptly.

"The name of the city or town that's closest to you," I said patiently.

"I reckon that'd be Cosby, but it's a right fur piece. I ain't been thar but onct since I married Burl."

"Do you live in Tennessee or North Carolina?"

"Tennessee, I reckon, but we hunt 'n fish on both sides. Some says they live in North C'lina."

"Some, *who*?" I asked.

"Some of Burl's people."

"Look," I said, with a flash of inspiration, "you get a bill for electricity. Does it come from Tennessee or North Carolina?"

"Ain't got no 'lectricity. We don't use nothin' we hafta depend on other folk fer. 'Cept coal oil [kerosene], and Burl gits that over to the highway."

"What highway is that?" I was beginning to see the futility of my questions.

"Don't know the number of it," she replied.

"Is your real name Mary Campbell?" I asked.

Her frightened glance told me the answer. Her pale eyes darted around the room, like an animal trapped in a box. I could well imagine her somewhere on the side of a mountain, cut off from the twentieth century.

"I need to make water," she said desperately.

"I'll send a nurse to take you to the bathroom." I had not heard *that* expression in years, either.

83

I went over to the employees' break area and got a cup of coffee. Sitting down, I lit a cigarette. In a few minutes the young doctor came in. He shook out a cigarette from a crumpled pack of Winstons.

"You shouldn't smoke," he said, lighting up, "especially not in a stressful profession like yours."

"That's what I hear."

"She tell you anything?" he asked.

"No, and . . ."

"Officer! Officer!" The young nurse who had taken the woman to the restroom ran around the corner. "That woman just ran out the side door. She insisted on taking her clothes to the bathroom and had them on when she ran past me."

I walked rapidly to the door and looked out. There were several hundred vehicles in a parking lot that covered an acre. Somewhere on the lot, I knew, was an old red pickup truck. Also, we were a short distance from a wooded area. I was sure she could run like a deer, even wounded. Certainly she could out-distance me. I went back to the break area.

"Doc, I don't think we'll ever know that woman's name. She's gone."

"Oh well, they probably couldn't pay the bill anyway," he sighed. "Thanks for coming."

"No problem. Thanks for the coffee."

As I left the parking lot a few minutes later, I saw an old red pickup pulling onto the highway. The truck had a taillight out, a clear violation, providing me a chance to satisfy my curiosity. My hand hovered over the blue light switch for a moment. Then I changed my mind.

I was fairly certain there would be a gunfight if I stopped the old truck. Those people, I knew, would not play by my rules. Where they came from, I was one of the bad guys. It was too high a price for satisfying my curiosity.

"Go on home," I thought. "We don't have anything else you need, anyway."

12

"Be Advised I Have a Gunship in Sight"

"**B**aker 9," the officer said, just before dawn one morning, "be advised I have a gunship in sight."

"Can you advise what kind of gunship you have in sight?" Good dispatchers are hard to rattle.

"It's big, propellers on both ends. It's landing at Farragut High School," he said. "I can't advise the make, as I am not familiar with helicopters."

"Ten–four, Baker 9. I'll check with the proper authorities on that gunship."

"Ten–four, dispatch, I'll be standing by."

As it turned out, the Secret Service was working on contingency plans for a planned visit by the President. They had not bothered to inform the Knox County Sheriff's Department, no doubt thinking that no one would notice a gunship landing in the early morning hours.

Most police work is fairly routine, but when something out of the ordinary happens, it sticks with you. A warm summer afternoon comes to mind.

"Baker 10, I'll be stopping a riding lawn mower driven by one white male subject. We'll be on Old Rutledge Pike in front of the heavy equipment place. It looks like a Snapper lawn mower."

"Ten–four, Baker 10. Did you advise in front of the heavy equipment place?"

"Ten–four."

All over the county, I knew that my shift mates would be whooping and hollering. I was already well known for my vigilance against drunk drivers.

As with most stories, there was more to it than met the eye.

I was sitting in the driveway of a closed business, munching a roast beef on dark, and sipping a coke. I paid little attention to the riding lawn mower the first time I saw it in a yard across the street.

Then I recognized the little girl who was perched on the driver's lap. I had seen her while responding to a domestic disturbance call the previous night shift. The little girl—four years old—had taken refuge with her mother in the same little market where I had bought the sandwich. The frightened child told me that her daddy had been hitting her mother. The woman refused to prosecute, forcing me to let it drop.

The second time I saw the lawn mower, it left the yard and pulled into the street heading east, the driver tilting his head to finish a can of beer. Throwing the beer can into the street, he drove away, the little girl still on his lap. It was growing dark, so I put away my sandwich and coke and followed to see if he was going to pull back off the road.

When the lawnmower continued for about a quarter of a mile, I hit the blue lights and tapped the siren. The man, small and wiry with stringy blond hair, looked startled but pulled over. I told the dispatcher what was going on.

"What's the matter, officer?" He tried to hide the contempt, but did not succeed.

"Well, for one thing, littering with your beer can back there. Mainly, though, I'm concerned about the safety of a little girl riding at dusk on a lawn mower without lights. Where are you headed, anyway?"

"Nowhere, just ridin'. I don't reckon it's against the law to ride around on a lawnmower with my own stepdaughter, is it?" The sarcasm broke through with full force.

"Yes, it is, for several reasons. Among them, you appear to be intoxicated, that vehicle is not licensed for road use, and you're endangering a child."

"This is a joke, right?" I saw then that he had an audience

to play to. The woman from the market, apparently his wife, and a stocky, shirtless man had walked up. "Supertrooper here doesn't like me drivin' my lawnmower in the road!" He swayed as he smiled a sneering grin.

"Step over there to level ground," I said. "I'm going to give you a field sobriety test."

"This has gone far enough. I'm gonna . . ."

"You're going to do exactly what I say, or I'm going to load you without a test. Do it now!"

"What can I do for you?" I asked the man who had walked up.

"That's my lawnmower," he said.

"Go get a truck and come after it. I'll have to get you to sign a release, though." He nodded and walked away.

"Can I take my little girl home?" the woman asked.

"Yes, but I hope never to see her in another dangerous situation of any kind. Understood?"

"Yes, officer." She left with the little girl waving over her shoulder, not even asking about her husband's fate.

The man did miserably on the field sobriety test. Later, at the jail, he blew a .13 percent on the intoximeter. A reading of .10 percent is the presumption level in Tennessee.

"So what are you charging me with, supertrooper?" he asked from the back of my cruiser.

"I could charge you with driving under the influence, but right now I'm considering a charge of public drunkenness. It upsets me that you were endangering the little girl."

"Driving under the influence? I'd like to see you do that, supertrooper! You'd be a joke in court." He laughed and sealed his fate.

I knew that under Tennessee law any motorized vehicle was covered by the statutes, but I had never heard of anyone being charged for drunk driving on a lawnmower. I also knew that the only exception to the requirement that a vehicle have a tag while upon the roads was agricultural equipment. I did not think the lawnmower would qualify as such.

I charged him with driving under the influence and violation of the state registration law. Since he had a prior conviction for driving under the influence, I made it a second offense charge, carrying a minimum of forty-five days in jail.

In court, a plea bargain was reached. The judge and attorney general agreed with me that the riding lawn mower was a motor vehicle, covered under the codes. As part of the plea bargain, the state dropped the charge of not having a tag, and the suspect pled guilty to driving under the influence. It had slipped my mind that I intended to charge him with littering.

That was the first and, to my knowledge, still the only conviction for drunk driving on a lawn mower in the state of Tennessee.

"Baker 10, check a suspicious subject. York Road, near Old Andersonville Pike. The complainant says a man in a strange vehicle has put some sort of electronic gear in her yard and is sitting in his car by the road."

"Ten–four," I said, wondering what kind of imaginary vision a member of the citizenry had conjured up. Cops spend a lot of time chasing shadows and noises. Suspicious vehicles usually turn out to be lovers or abandoned cars.

Rounding a curve, I saw the vehicle and killed the lights. Watching, I could see that inside a station wagon, with the dome lights on, a man appeared to be engrossed in watching a piece of equipment. A satellite dish had been set up on a hill in the front yard of a house. Cables ran from the dish to the car.

Suddenly, *my* imagination was running rampant. The Iran/Iraq war was waging wide open, and Libya was making threats. And I could see that he was dark-skinned, with black hair and a pencil thin mustache.

"Sheriff's department," I announced. "I need to speak with you."

He glanced up, momentarily startled, then went back to the equipment he was watching. "Yes, but make it brief. I am very busy." English was obviously a second language.

"What are you doing?" I asked.

"Tracking satellites," he said.

Brazen, I decided.

"Who gave you permission to put that satellite dish in the yard up there?"

"It's all taken care of. Not to worry about it," he answered.

Annoyed, I called the dispatcher. "Call the complainant and see if they've given anyone permission to set up equipment in their yard. Also, have them switch their porch light on so that I can be certain I'm in the right place."

A moment later the porch light came on. "Baker 10, the complainant says no one has permission to be there and that no one else has authority to give that permission."

"All right, pack up and get moving," I told the man. "But first, I need some identification."

"Sorry," the man said matter of factly, "but I'm at a crucial point. I can't move right now."

"My friend, you have trespassed and are trespassing on private property. I have politely spoken, but now I am telling you, flat out, point blank, without equivocation. Show me some identification, and start loading your equipment!"

He handed me a driver's license and angrily began to load his equipment while muttering under his breath. I ran his tag and driver's license, but found nothing wrong.

"What nationality are you?" I asked.

"Palestinian," he snapped, slamming the rear of the station wagon closed. I watched him drive away angrily.

Later I talked to my lieutenant, who was also an old friend and schoolmate. "Only you, Hunter," he shook his head, "could find an Arab on York Road, in the heart of East Tennessee, tracking satellites in the middle of the night."

"There is a memo," the captain said, "from the front office. The county has hired a firm to help them in drawing up new maps. You may find individuals in strange places, tracking satellites. As long as they are not blocking the road, and have permission from landowners, they are not to be disturbed."

He looked directly at me as he was talking. Snickering broke out around the room. A few nights later I came in and found a "Junior G–Man" kit in front of my seat at roll call. It was complete with badge, gun, and secret decoder ring.

When my next unusual experience happened, I was a little reluctant about broadcasting it, needless to say. However, you cannot keep some things quiet, no matter how you try.

It had rained just after midnight. My window was rolled down and my air conditioner was off so that I could smell the aroma of wet earth as I cruised down a back road, making a final sweep of my beat before daylight.

Suddenly, in the dark I met a golf cart going in the opposite direction. On the golf cart was a man in a white dinner jacket, with one arm around a woman in a white gown.

For a moment, I thought I was hallucinating. Then I locked up the brakes, sliding to a stop. In the rearview mirror, I could see the golf cart continuing on its way. Putting the car in reverse, I backed up until I was within range. Then I stopped and yelled from my car window.

"Pull over to the side of road." The golf cart gave a burst of speed. "I mean it. You'd better stop!"

Picking up the mike, I started to call for a unit to cut off the golf cart at the next intersection but thought better of it.

I had no place to turn around, so I continued driving backward, yelling at the people on the golf cart. In essence, I was involved in a backward pursuit with a golf cart at speeds reaching ten miles per hour. I was afraid to back around the golf cart—though I could have—fearing I would hit them.

Finally I came to an abandoned wagon road with enough space to turn around. Turning, I saw the couple watching me, their faces white in my headlights. Before I could get to them, they jumped from the golf cart and ran into the woods.

Perhaps I was not dedicated enough to chase them through the wet fields and woods, or perhaps I simply did not *want* to arrest anyone for possession of a stolen golf cart. In any case, they were gone.

The name of the only country club with a golf course in the entire area was on the cart. Going to the secondary channel, I called for a wrecker with a dolly. In a short while, we had the golf cart back at the country club.

"There was a big bash here earlier," the security guard said. "Probably a couple of tanked up guests."

They had covered about seven miles before encountering me and were apparently heading back to return the cart. It was seven miles in pitch dark, on a cloudy night.

All cops know that strange things happen on the streets at night. Some are even stranger than others, though.

13

"The Car Will Be a Salmon Color"

There is not a human being alive who has not blurted out something that they immediately wish they had not said. One incident that quickly comes to mind is President Jimmy Carter's referring to ex-Vice-president Hubert Humphrey as "Hubert Horatio Hornblower" in a nationally televised speech. God only knows what the President had on his mind at the time.

Cops also make their share of blunders on the air. When they do this, they find out how many people monitor police radios, including the press.

When cops blunder, they sometimes have a dispatcher perfectly willing to assist them in looking like idiots. Hanging around the police infects dispatchers with a sense of humor akin to that of officers.

A few years ago, one of my shiftmates was given this call: "Check a horse. The complainant advises it will be running through Stonecrest Subdivision." Even in East Tennessee, with its many rural areas, it is not a common thing to find horses running through subdivisions. There is, however, a riding stable within a short distance of this particular area in Knoxville.

Most officers keep a pad and pen on the seat next to them, or attached to the dash, for notes. When the call came through, my shiftmate picked up his pen to jot down the information and without thinking, asked the next logical question. At least, it would have been logical if he were looking for a person or a vehicle.

"Did the complainant advise a description of the horse?" he asked, pen poised over paper.

"That's a negative," the dispatcher replied without hesitation. "Turn into Stonecrest Subdivision. It'll be the first horse you come to."

An Atlanta police officer was dispatched to a shooting call late one evening. As it was being given out, so was a call concerning a woman in labor. Because of the heavy radio traffic, the officer thought he had been given the pregnant woman to check on.

Generally, in the case of pregnant women there is plenty of time after an officer arrives to get an ambulance to the scene. As the Atlanta officer arrived, however, he saw the crowd gathered around a woman lying in the middle of the sidewalk. She was lying there because she had been shot in the foot.

The officer, however, was still under the impression that he had been dispatched to check on a woman in labor. Seeing her on the ground, he decided that it was too late for an ambulance. That is why the officer got out of the car, trotted up the sidewalk in front of a hundred housing project residents, and yelled, "Has anybody taken her panties off yet?"

A few years ago in Knoxville, an accident involving a livestock truck en route to a slaughter house happened during rush hour traffic, right in front of a fast food restaurant. Pigs and hogs of all sizes were running up and down the street, squealing and causing pandemonium. Local high school kids were adding to the confusion by chasing the pigs.

At some point in the confusion, a large hog darted in front of a car and was hit. It lay in the street, mortally wounded, addings its strident squeals to the confusion and blocking a lane of traffic.

Out in the county, injured animals are not so much of a problem. Generally, permission can be obtained to put them out of their misery quickly. Not so inside the city. There are too many people nearby to risk firing a weapon, no matter how badly the animal is hurt. Knowing he would need a veterinarian to put the animal out of its misery, one of the officers called the dispatcher.

"Call the university," he said, "and tell them we're gonna need one of their people out here to give an injection. I've got an injured pig down in the street."

"Ten–four," the dispatcher shot back, "can you advise which *officer* has been hurt?" The officer, I am sure, flinched and prepared himself for the merciless attacks of his brother officers.

One story, a favorite of mine, has been handed down from the days before all police and emergency lines were recorded. Dispatchers were a little more liberal with their sarcasm then; they could always say they were misunderstood by irate complainants, or simply deny an accusation.

One crusty old dispatcher, I am told, had received about twenty calls one night from the same woman. She claimed that her ex-husband was harassing her by phone, threatening to come to her house. When the final call came in, interrupting the dispatcher's dinner for the third time, the woman told the dispatcher that her husband was breaking down the front door. He immediately dispatched a cruiser and informed the woman that help was on the way.

"What should I do until they get here?" she asked.

"Lady," he said in exasperation, "if you're afraid, the only thing I can tell you is to shoot the son of a bitch!" His eyes widened in terror moments later as the sound of shots being fired echoed in his ears.

He experienced a terrifying few minutes until the cruiser arrived on the scene and he was informed that the woman had missed with all shots. He had already been mentally composing the report in which he would try to explain why a woman had killed her husband on direct orders from the Sheriff's Department.

An Illinois cop passed this little saga on to me at a conference a couple of years ago. He says a call came in the evening hours, resulting in a patrolman's being dispatched to a suburban area to look for a white dog that had escaped from an open front door.

Cops hate such calls, complaining that they can never get any *real* police work done when they are tied up on trivial, nonpolice assignments. Obviously irritated, the cop took the call. Most modern departments dispatch a car on all citizen complaints, both for public relations and to head off possible liabilities.

In a few minutes the angry cop announced that he was in the area. He asked for a description of the house and a repeat on the street number. About five minutes later, he called the dispatcher, sounding a little upset.

"Car 7, do you have a number to call the complainant back?"

"Ten–four," the dispatcher replied. "I'm dialing now."

"Car 7, ask the complainant if her dog is white with one black ear."

"Ten–four, car 7, the complainant says that's her dog."

"Car 7, I'm about six houses east of the complainant. Advise her I just ran over her dog," the officer said with great reluctance.

A few years ago I was dispatched to an emergency clinic to sign the chart on an animal bite. All animal bites in Tennessee must be reported to the police. Usually the animal involved is a dog or a cat, but this particular call concerned a domestic rabbit. A visiting child had opened the cage and had attempted to pick up a large rabbit. The child had been scratched and nipped, though not seriously. The rabbit had run away.

"I'll be clear," I told the dispatcher, "report executed on a rabbit bite."

"Did you advise a *rabbit?*" the dispatcher replied. It was a slow night, so I picked it up.

"Ten–four. The assailant rabbit will be about a year old, weighs approximately six pounds, is brown and white with a white tail, and answers to the name of Fluffy. Approach with caution."

The dispatcher then proceeded to issue a countywide alert for the rabbit. I had to pull over and laugh, hoping all the time that no big brass were listening.

The only thing more fun for a dispatcher than stinging a cop who is not staying on his toes is stinging a cop who has no sense of humor. A humorless cop is a rare breed, but they do exist.

One such officer worked for the department a few years

ago. Self-importance literally oozed from him as he walked about doing his John Wayne act. At six feet, three inches, he looked like a recruiting poster cop, but all who worked around him knew him to be an overgrown crybaby.

After being transferred off his regular beat, he set out to make life miserable for everyone. He insisted that he had no idea of the layout of his new beat, and the dispatchers had to check the map on every call they gave him. He requested a supervisor on every trivial assignment, obviously believing that if he complained enough, he could get his old beat back.

About six hours into his shift, he began to tell the dispatcher that he could not hear the radio because of static, making the dispatcher repeat everything several times. She waited patiently, however, until he finally set himself up, as she knew he would.

"Baker 12," he said in a nasal, grating voice. "I still can't hear properly. Can you advise if there's a whining sound in my radio?"

"That's a negative, Baker 12. *The whine is all in your voice.*"

There were no further problems from him that day.

"I'll be stopping a vehicle at Quincy and Blake," the officer said to the dispatcher. The car will be a salmon color."

All over Knoxville, cops were saying, "*Salmon color?*" This was followed by an immediate outburst of laughter, during which every cop in town looked up the nearest officer and asked, "Did you just hear what he said? A *salmon* color!"

I am sure the officer realized what he had done, even before he ran into the first cop, who reminded him with much hooting and giggling. Why he said it, I do not know. Maybe he and his wife had been looking at paint samples. For the next week, though, cops all over the county were stopping *fuchsia* cars, *aquamarine* cars, *mauve* cars, *champagne* cars, and *ocher* cars.

I am told the officer who stopped the *salmon* colored car went around in an *ebony* depression for several days, with a case of the *cobalt* blues. Cops are relentless.

It happens to you, though, when you least expect it. The code in Knox County used to cancel a call is "10–22." One night, while en route to an open door call, another officer arrived ahead of me and notified the dispatcher that a cleaning crew was in the building, not burglars. An officer must continue on any call given him, however, until cancelled. So fi-

95

nally, receiving no cancellation, I said impatiently, "Baker 10, shall I continue on, or shall I *twen–tenny-two?*"

Realizing that my tongue had tied on the last sentence, I desperately tried to correct it. It was too late, though. Before I could key the mike, the dispatcher drilled me.

"Just twen-tenny-two, Baker 10. *Twen–tenny-two,*" she emphasized sweetly.

14

Roly-poly and the Little Dog

Detective Mike Blake (not his real name) of the Knox County Sheriff's Department is a man at ease with himself. His eyes almost always have the proverbial twinkle, just waiting to break into laughter. You do not call a cop "Roly-poly" or "Booba" unless he *is* laid back, comfortable with what he is. Mike answers to both nicknames.

About five feet, seven inches tall (his weight is confidential), going bald on top, Blake tends toward roundness. He enjoys good food and good jokes, both with equal gusto. Sidling up to you wearing the expression of a mischievous little boy, he will begin, "Did you hear the one about . . ."

Blake has been a cop for a long time. He has nothing to prove to anyone and no apparent animosity toward the world. He did his time on the streets in uniform and now is happy to leave it to the kids. He is highly thought of by veterans and rookies; veterans know he paid his dues, and he never talks down to rookies.

At times, however, Booba can be a trial for training officers and supervisors. For instance, during a surprise inspection of his cruiser he was once found to be short of equipment. To be specific, he had no flashlight, handcuffs, or extra ammunition in the car.

This led Bill Fox, the chief deputy, to ask him if he was still playing on the same team as the rest of us.

97

Unshaken by the inspection, Booba told me later that things were not as bad as they seemed because (1) he arrests only white collar criminals (working forgery and bad checks) who need no handcuffs; (2) working only by day, a flashlight is useless; (3) being such a superb marksman, he needed no extra ammunition.

During a course being taught by a training officer, Blake once reduced the entire class (except for the training officer) to hysterics with his backhanded logic. The class dealt with the reasons for accidents involving cruisers. The training officer explained that accidents are caused by many different factors. He named stress, anxiety, and anger as being responsible for some accidents, then asked the class to join in and give him other possible causes. Booba's hand shot up.

With a lift of the eyebrows, knowing that Booba had seldom shown any interest in his classes, the training officer told him to speak out.

"I have found," Blake said, his balding forehead wrinkling into what appeared to be a solemn expression, "that *hunger* can cause automobile accidents."

The training officer sat staring for a moment. He knew that Booba was about to make him uncomfortable but saw no way out. After all, he *had* asked the question.

"All right," he said reluctantly. "How can hunger cause accidents?"

"Well," Mike said with a cherubic smile, "one time I was drivin' down Kingston Pike in real heavy traffic, and I was hungry. I was comin' to Pizza Hut and thought I might stop and eat. So I looked over to see how crowded the parking lot was. While I was lookin' out the window, I hit another car in the ass-end. The accident was caused by hunger." He nodded his head and pursed his lips for emphasis, keeping a straight face.

A few seconds passed before his words sank in. The class erupted in guffaws of laughter. The training officer sat quietly until it ended, then went on with as much dignity as he could muster under the circumstances.

Not all of Booba's humor is verbal. He is not above what some people might call crude jokes; for instance, the novelty shop item that came in a bottle labeled "Instant Farts."

Easing up next to an unsuspecting fellow employee on some

pretext, Blake liberally doused him from behind. For the rest of the morning, the man noticed that people were shying away from him but did not know why—not until some blunt cop told him exactly what he smelled like.

A little detective work led him back to Booba, who was still snickering maliciously and telling everyone who would listen to "go smell of Bobby."

Booba took it pretty well when the victim exacted revenge. It just so happened that the object of Bobba's prank was in charge of fleet management and had a key to all cruisers. He searched out Blake's vehicle [so I am told] early one morning and parked it in the chief deputy's private parking spot, leaving the roly-poly detective to explain why he had done the unthinkable.

Yes, Mike Blake is a hard man to rattle, but even he has moments when the proper words cannot be found.

Such a time came as Booba worked a larceny one evening

"You wouldn't believe the kind of week I've had," the complainant said.

Mike listened sympathetically as the woman unfolded her story.

The week had started off, she told him, with her husband filing for divorce, without warning. Then a tree in her backyard was blown over, damaging a neighbor's house. As she was attempting to cope with those problems, her house caught on fire. Her son had to be rushed to the hospital suffering from smoke inhalation. Meanwhile, neighbors carried her furniture out on the patio to prevent smoke damage. At the hospital with her son, she passed out. It was discovered that she had kidney stones, so she was hospitalized for three days. During that time, thieves stole her furniture from the patio.

"Well," she said philosophically, "my son is all right, and nothing happened to my little dog. I guess I should be thankful for *that*."

Mike filled in the blanks on the offense report, nodding sympathetically. With 80 percent or more of burglaries going unsolved nationally, sympathy is generally the only thing a burglary detective can give.

The woman thanked Booba as he left, both for the report

and for his sympathetic ear. He climbed into his cruiser, pondering the woman's streak of bad luck.

"It was a *real* steep driveway," Blake told me with a pained expression. "I put the car in reverse and rolled back. There was a sort of thump-thump sound, and I got out to see what I had run over."

A few minutes later, he reluctantly knocked on the door of the house he had just left. When the woman opened the door, she appeared puzzled.

"Ma'am," Blake said, staring at his feet, "you know that little dog of yours . . . ?"

It was quiet for a moment. Then a horrible expression passed over her face as she put two and two together.

"You *didn't?*" she asked in disbelief.

"Yes, ma'am. I'm afraid I've run over your little dog."

15

To Err Is Human

The little man walked toward me with a determined stride, his face set for conflict. I had never seen him before, but I knew what was coming. He had a bone to pick with me, with any cop who could not get away and would have to be pleasant.

I fit both categories that morning. My cruiser, shined and polished for the occasion, was parked in the center of a busy shopping mall. As an instructor for the DUI (driving under the influence) enforcement unit, I was there to demonstrate the breath testing equipment and to answer questions asked by citizens.

"Excuse me, officer, but I have a question." He was about fifty, the type of individual who might be called "cadaverous" by a mystery writer. His expression was prim and self-righteous.

"Yes, sir?"

"Is it true that diabetics sometimes go into a state resembling intoxication and that their breath will give an odor similar to alcoholic beverages?" I could tell that he knew the answer.

"That's true," I replied, "but this breath testing unit can tell the difference. Acetone, which is given off by a diabetic's breath, will not be read by this machine."

"But," he turned to look at the four or five people standing nearby, "if he wasn't tested, if he was arrested for public drunkenness, a diabetic could be jailed for being drunk when he wasn't. Right?"

"That could happen," I answered, "and probably has."

"So you admit that innocent people get thrown into jail?" He looked around triumphantly.

"No, sir. I said that mistakes happen."

"Do you fire an incompetent police officer when he arrests an innocent person?" His eyes were positively glowing.

"That would not indicate incompetence. Medical people have to test the diabetic's blood to make a diagnosis in such cases. Also, diabetics generally carry identification or tell you they're diabetic."

"Well, I call it incompetence! I call it an outrage when an innocent person is jailed. It's fascism, plain and simple!"

At that point, I signaled a mall security officer. Moments later, he was escorting the protesting man away. I never knew what incident had keyed the man's rage. On one point, however, he was correct. Policemen make mistakes, not as often as the little man probably believed, but more often than cops like to think about.

"Be on the lookout," the dispatcher rasped over the airways, "for a 10–52 suspect." I was immediately alert. Ten–fifty-two is the Knox County code for armed robbery. "The suspect will be a white male, heavyset, beard, dark brown hair. He will be wearing a denim jacket, blue jeans, and a red ball cap. Suspect was last seen driving a green pickup truck, GMC or Chevrolet, late model, with a taillight out. Ten–fifty-two occurred approximately fifteen minutes ago. Suspect is armed with a semiautomatic pistol."

I wrote down the description and pulled out into traffic from the lot where I had been parked. Approaching a well-lit area along the two-lane road, I saw a dark green pickup truck coming toward me.

The truck was driven by a bearded white male wearing a red ball cap. Looking in the rearview mirror, my heart began to pound. There was a taillight out on the truck. I wheeled around in the road and fell in behind him.

"Baker 10, start a back-up unit. I think I have the suspect vehicle from the armed robbery." I gave her my location.

"Baker 10, all north units are tied up. I'll start a west car toward you." That put back-up maybe fifteen minutes away.

Every cop dreams of being in the right place at the right

time. Unlike in the movies, real-life cops seldom drive up on armed robberies. The patrolman's general fare is the misdemeanor arrest. There was no way I was going to let the suspect evade me. We were minutes from the county line and the reach of my radio.

"Baker 10, I can't wait on back-up. I'm going to take him down." I gave her the intersection, loosened my shotgun in the rack, and hit the blue lights, prepared for a chase or a shooting confrontation.

The man glanced nervously into the mirror and tapped the brakes. Moments later, he eased onto the shoulder. Quickly stepping out, shotgun in my right hand, I spoke over the address system.

"You in the truck, raise your hands where I can see them. Do it now!"

The man's hands rose jerkily.

"Remove the keys from the ignition with your *left* hand, keeping the right hand in sight. Drop the keys out the window. Do it now!"

"With your *right* hand, reach out and open the door from the outside."

"Step out of the truck slowly. Keep your hands up and your back to me. Do it now!"

As the man stepped shakily from the truck, I pitched the microphone into the seat. He could now hear me without the public address system. I leveled the shotgun at his back.

"Put your hands behind your head and lace your fingers. Walk backward toward me, slowly. Do it now!"

"Drop slowly to your knees. Cross one leg over the other. If you make any sudden moves, I'll shoot. Do it now!"

"Baker 10," the radio grunted.

I took the portable from its clip, still holding the shotgun on the suspect. "Go ahead."

"The 10–52 suspect has been picked up just across the county line. Repeat. The suspect is in custody. The weapon and money have been recovered."

"Ten–four," I replied, wondering what to say to a citizen with a shotgun pointed at his back.

"Sir, excuse me."

"Yeah," he gasped.

103

"There has been a case of mistaken identity here. If you'll stand up, I'll explain it to you."

He nodded, unfolded his legs, and rose shakily. Walking to the front of my cruiser, he put both hands on the hood and began to breathe deeply.

"You fit the description of an armed robbery suspect, right down to the ball cap. I know that you're upset. If you want to complain, I'll understand perfectly."

"No," he took another deep breath. "Mistakes happen. I'm just glad it's over." He turned and looked at me.

"I know it was frightening," I told him.

"It really was. I'd been meanin' to fix that taillight. I thought that was why you stopped me. Damn if it didn't seem a little extreme for a taillight, though."

When he was gone, I pulled behind a shopping center and laughed hysterically, to ease the tension. The idea of a shotgun being used on traffic offenders was just too ludicrous.

The rain was coming at the windshield in walls, making visibility difficult. A drunken prisoner was mumbling in the back seat, and a patrolman from another shift was riding with me, killing time and bemoaning the fact that his wife had left him.

The truck came at me from the left, running a red light. Swerving to the shoulder, I barely avoided being hit. The truck wobbled on up the road as if nothing had happened. I hit the blue lights and siren and called it in.

After about two blocks, the driver seemed to notice the blue lights. He pulled over to the shoulder. "No use in both of us getting soaked," I told the patrolman. "I'll check him."

I approached the driver's side, rain saturating every pore of my body within seconds. "Step out of the truck!"

The driver, a chunky man in checkered flannel shirt, did not move. I raised on my tiptoes until I could see that both his hands were empty. It is the hands that kill. I opened the door, watching his hands.

"Step out," I told him.

Without warning, his hand dropped to his right hip pocket. There was a distinct metallic clink. *Pistol*, I thought! A cop's nightmare. An armed suspect, too close to retreat, too close to draw a weapon.

I went berserk.

My only thought was to keep him from turning to shoot me. I grabbed him by the hair and shoulder and jerked him bodily from the cab, slamming him into the side of the truck.

"Drop it!" I yelled, once more slamming his right arm into the side of the vehicle. He grunted from the impact, but said nothing. I waited for the sound of gunshots.

From the corner of my eye, I could see my partner dancing around, trying to get a shot at the suspect. He had no doubt in his mind that I was grappling with an armed suspect.

"Don't shoot!" I shouted, fearing that he would hit me.

Finally, the man's right hand dropped into my view. There was no weapon in it. Pushing him upright against the side of the truck, I saw a leather biker's wallet hanging from a chain attached to his belt. He had reached for the wallet, and the metallic sound had come from the links of the chain rubbing together. The wallet was open, and everything in it had dropped to the pavement. All the paper, money and all, washed into the gulley as I stood there too exhausted to move.

"Wha's goin' on here?" the drunk and battered man asked as the rain ran in rivulets from his face.

An hour later, as I sat booking the first prisoner, I heard the man with the wallet on the phone talking to a family member. His blood alcohol was three times the legal limit, which was why he had difficulty understanding even simple sentences.

"Come and bail me out in the mornin'," he said, watching me through red-rimmed eyes. "An' I'll tell ya somethin', don't drink an' drive in this county. By God, I've never seen cops handle drunk drivers the way they do."

I was cruising through a nearby city, enjoying the drive. My evening had been spent visiting a friend I had not seen in a long while. A siren bleated behind me, the sound that comes from bumping the siren button, rather than turning it on. I saw blue lights in my rearview mirror.

Glancing at my speedometer, I saw that I was a little over the speed limit. I chuckled to myself. It was a slow night, I decided, if cops were stopping people for such trivial offenses. Slow nights happen, though. I pulled over, planning to share a laugh with the patrolman.

Watching my side mirror, I saw that the man easing along

the side of my car was not in uniform. I also noticed that he was approaching *very* carefully, much more so than is normal on a traffic stop.

That was when I looked in the rearview mirror and saw the uniformed patrol officer. He had a twelve-gauge pump pointed at the back of my head. My mouth went dry.

"Hand me your driver's license, over your shoulder." The voice was gruff and had none of the routine courtesy about it.

"Officer?" I croaked out.

"What?"

"Before I reach into my right hip pocket, I think you should know that I'm a cop and that there's a .357 magnum on the seat beside me. I don't want to make you nervous—not with that shotgun pointed at me."

"Then maybe you'd better get out. Open your door the *proper* way and step out with your hands where I can see them."

Reaching across my chest with my right hand, I opened the door with the outside door handle. That is the *proper* way. The detective had stepped back and assumed a firing crouch.

Stepping out slowly, I turned so he could see that there were no weapons. Cautiously, I removed my badge case and flipped it open. The detective relaxed somewhat, but not entirely.

"Take a look," the detective said to the patrolman, who walked toward us.

"No, that's not him. The suspect is tall and blond."

"Sorry for the inconvenience, officer. We just had an armed robbery. The guy was driving a car like this with Knox County plates. I know you understand that."

They drove off without further adieu. Indeed, I did understand that. I still sat shivering for several minutes before I could continue on. Sometimes it is good to see things from the other side.

Mistakes do happen. At such times, we should try to remember: to err is human and to forgive . . . well, sometimes that's the *only* thing you can do.

16

"Come on, Man, Give Me a Break"

Cops learn to thrive on the absurd. They have to. A humorless cop is a person well on the way to a nervous breakdown. Every cop also has had the experience of telling a story, after which looks of horror passed over the faces of everyone in the room.

It is the sense of the absurd, however, that gets a cop through situations that other people will never encounter. How many people, for instance, ever deal with suicide? Cops do it all the time, and it would be unbearable without a coping mechanism. For instance, consider the man who called 911 and said that he had shot himself.

The two officers arrived and approached the silent house cautiously. Whether they have been dispatched on a suicide call or a murder call, if a weapon is involved, cops approach cautiously. Suicidal people with guns may turn their rage outward.

Inside, they saw two trails of blood. Through a bathroom door, they saw a mirror with blood smeared all over it. It was obvious that one trail of blood led to the bathroom and one away. Someone had apparently stood looking into the mirror. The two trails ended in the living room.

Approaching cautiously, they stepped through the door. A man sat in an easy chair, his hand over a bloody scalp wound.

He was soaked with blood. The ceiling above was splattered with blood, and there was a bullet hole. Angling the pistol at his temple, the man had fired a nine millimeter pistol. The bullet had entered the scalp, turned on the bone, and exited without doing any serious damage.

As they stood surveying the scene, the man looked up at them and spoke, a pained expression on his face.

"Man, I've got a headache like you wouldn't *believe.*"

We walked up on the rickety wooden porch and peered through a dirty window pane. A neighbor coming home from the late shift had noticed the light on and was unable to get the old man to the door.

"He's never up past eleven," the woman said, "and he won't come to the door. I'm afraid something has happened to him. There's a phone by his bed. He would have called for help, if he was able. This man is eighty-two years old."

The neighbor stood by the road watching, as we peered through the window. "I see a pair of feet," my partner said. "They don't appear to be moving."

"I guess we'd better go in," I said reluctantly. Cops hate to break through doors. If they turn out to be wrong, the damage has to be justified.

Fortunately, the old door gave without too much damage; the locking mechanism was weak and easily slipped over the plate. We walked slowly through the bedroom door where the feet were visible.

An old man looked up from the floor beside the bed, a sheen of sweat on his face, white hair pasted to his forehead. He laid down a Bible, which he had been reading.

"Are you all right, sir?" I asked.

"*No,* I broke my hip as I was gittin' into bed, about eight o'clock," he said irritably.

I shuddered at the thought of lying for seven hours on a cold floor with a broken hip. Quickly we called for an ambulance, then got blankets from a hall closet to warm him. As we put the blankets over him, I noticed that the telephone was within reaching distance.

"Sir, is your telephone out of order?"

"No, it works fine," he replied.

"Why didn't you call for help?"

"Well, everyone I know is too old to get out, except my next door neighbor, and she works nights."

"Why didn't you call for an ambulance or the police?"

"Well, son," he said, as if I were simple minded, "there hadn't been any laws broke and I was gonna call for an ambulance when they opened in the morning. Hardly any business opens before seven."

My partner and I strode for the door, controlling ourselves until we were outside before bursting into gales of laughter. The neighbor, who had rushed by as we came out, came to the door and glared at us.

"I'm glad you see the humor in an old man's suffering," she snapped at us. "You'll be old and feeble some day, you know."

We tried to explain, but only laughed harder every time we came to the part about waiting until the ambulance service "opened."

You had to be there.

The young black man had walked confidently into the records section of the Knox County Sheriff's Department, apparently with a flawed idea of how criminal records are kept. He had a form from a local security company to be filled out by records.

He had applied for work as a security guard, which required a background check from the sheriff's department. Later speculation was that since his arrests had all been through the city police, he did not expect the sheriff's department to know anything about them. No one ever asked him what was going through his mind, however.

The startled clerk immediately saw that he was a convicted felon, several times over. It was not his history that caused her mouth to drop open, but the fact that there was an outstanding warrant for armed robbery on file. The clerk immediately began to hunt for an officer.

Finding a cop at a police station is not always as easy as it sounds. Most cops do not work *at* police stations but spend their time in the field. Those who are assigned to the building may be at lunch or on break at any given time.

Apparently the man noticed that something was wrong. As an old convict, he no doubt understood body language well. For whatever reason, he fled down the hallway, leaving the paperwork behind.

Minutes later, officers were looking for him, but he was gone. A civilian out front gave a description of the car he had entered, and it was immediately broadcast to all units, city and county.

As the description of the car and suspect was being broadcast, Knox County patrolman Larry Hunter was on his way to work. One street over from the sheriff's department, he looked up and saw the suspect vehicle in front of him. He immediately called for back-up, then hit the siren.

There was nowhere to go in the heavy traffic, so the suspect surrendered. Moments later, the officer had him on the ground, cuffing and searching him.

Larry sat in his cruiser, waiting for the wrecker and doing his preliminary paperwork.

"What's the warrant for this time?" the prisoner asked.

"Armed robbery," Larry answered.

"Sheeit! I ain't robbed nobody."

"If you're innocent, you'll walk on the charge," Larry said with a shrug.

"Yeah, but I can't make the kind of bail they put on armed robbery. Man I can't believe it. There goes *another* summer!"

My brother Larry related another incident that left me in stitches. A former DUI enforcement officer, he has kept up his certification. One night as he was booking a prisoner, homicide brought in a man who had just killed someone.

"Larry," the homicide detective said, "the I.D. officer is busy. How about gettin' me a breath sample from this guy."

Such things as the sobriety of a suspect often are relevant when prosecuting a homicide. In this case, there was no doubt who had done the killing. It was a matter of degree.

The suspect, who was exceedingly drunk, went cooperatively to take the breath test. He had been through it before.

"How high do you think I'll go?" the man asked, slurring his words.

"Pretty high," Larry answered, preparing the machine.

"I went pretty high the las' time. How high do you think I'll go?"

"I don't know. Maybe into the midtwenties." A good technician can predict pretty close after he gives enough tests, and Larry is one of the best.

In a drunk driving case, the level of alcohol in the bloodstream has a lot of effect on the severity of punishment. Usually, the higher the blood alcohol level, the more severe the sentence. In a murder case, however, where a suspect is looking at a possible life sentence or even the death penalty, it is only incidental.

Apparently, though, this particular suspect was a little confused about the reason for his arrest.

"*Midtwennies?* Maybe I better not take this tes'."

"It's up to you," Larry said, "but if you're going to take it, blow into this tube."

"Oh, all right." The man took the tube and blew vigorously. When he was finished, the digital read-out began to click off. It quickly rose to .20 percent (.10 percent is the legal presumption level) and continued to go up. When it reached .26 percent, the murder suspect turned blearily to Larry.

"Come on, man," he said with great concern and sincerity, "*give me a break.*"

17

All the World's a Stage

Shakespeare was right. The world is a stage and the inhabitants are actors. Living in Elizabethan England, however, the bard could not have envisioned the sheer scale of the stage upon which twentieth-century Americans would play—television and movies.

Shakespeare had to get his audiences out to the Globe Theater. Today the stage is piped into the home. One can enjoy everything from situation comedies to . . . well, Shakespeare, without leaving the house.

Events once slow in making their way across continents are now beamed at the speed of light. Teenage boys in California start walking around with their suspenders dangling from their waists on Monday (God only knows why), and the peer group in Knoxville, Tennessee, is doing it on Tuesday.

There is hardly such a thing now as a local dialect. Appalachian people hear the same phrases on television as their counterparts in New York. A good phrase catches on like wildfire across the nation: for instance, Clint Eastwood's words in *Dirty Harry*, uttered while pointing a .44 magnum at his suspect, "Go ahead, *make my day.*"

Not only did this phrase catch on with the general public, but cops loved it. Training officers had to explain to street officers, that while the phrase was great drama, actually *saying* it to a suspect you might have to shoot could raise hostility in jurors who would later hear evidence in the case.

Cops are as susceptible to a good phrase as anyone else. In Joseph Wambaugh's novel *The Choirboys*, several drunk cops were sitting around trying to come up with a word disgusting enough to describe the street trash with whom they had daily contact. After discarding such old standbys as *dirt-bag*, *asshole*, and *scumbag*, they hit upon the word *scrote*, a derivative of *scrotum*. Soon after the publication of the book, cops all over the country had adopted the word. It is still in use. Citizens will not hear it. It is a word used only among the fraternity of bluesuits and badges.

Neither are criminals immune from aping their heroes.

"Put your hands on the car and spread your legs," my brother Larry told the young black man. "You are under arrest for driving under the influence."

"Now, hear this, bro'. I happen to know you cain't just be stoppin' a man for no reason. Why'd you stop me?"

There are four errors in the above statement: (1) He did not immediately assume the position as instructed; (2) He addressed the officer by a familiar term. Cops hate to be called bro', buddy, hey man, or any term of endearment; (3) He attempted to instruct the officer in the complexities of the law; and (4) He asked what he had done after it had already been explained to him.

"I've already explained everything to you. You are under arrest. Put your hands on the car and spread your legs, *now*."

"I ain't goin' to jail, bro'. Don't try to jump me. I been trained." He immediately assumed a karate stance (or what he thought was a karate stance) reminiscent of a generation of martial arts movies. His head was bouncing, the light reflecting off his dark glasses. He was *cool*.

Momentarily startled, Larry waited for the punch line. When none was forthcoming, he sighed deeply. "Look, do as I say. I don't want to hurt you. You're going to jail, one way or another."

"We'll see about that. *Kee-yi!*" he screamed, flicking out his right fist.

Blocking the right arm and stepping in, Larry drove home a devastating solar plexus punch with his left fist, then slammed the open palm of his right hand against the young man's jaw-

114

line. He hit the ground like a sack of potatoes. Larry rolled him over, cuffed him, and stuffed him in the car.

Apparently the young man had not wasted all his time watching martial arts movies, though. At some point it seems he had picked up a few educational programs, perhaps Dr. Joyce Brothers or another psychologist. As Larry sat in the cruiser doing his paperwork, the young man spoke to him in a quiet, respectful voice.

"Officer, you have a lot of stress in your job, don't you?"

The call went out as a 10–85, "disturbance in progress." The officer entered the dingy, badly lit bar and found the crowd backed up around the walls, watching a tall, gangly redhead of perhaps twenty. He was staggering about drunkenly, challenging the other patrons to fight.

"Come on," he yelled, "one a' you pansies try me out. Let's get it on." It was obvious that he was under the sway of old time movie brawls. It was also obvious everyone was in a mellow mood, except him. A fight is one thing you can almost always find in a bar.

"All right, pal. Enough!" the officer yelled above his screams. "You're under arrest for being publicly drunk. Put your hands on the bar and spread your legs."

He turned slowly and blinked to focus his eyes, apparently aware of the officer for the first time. Swaying, he smiled. "So you think its gonna be *that* easy, huh? Well, nobody takes me easy!"

The drunken redhead reached over and snatched a long necked beer bottle from the bar and stood holding it dramatically. The officer's hand dropped to his weapon, but he did not draw.

"Put the bottle down before someone gets hurt," the officer said calmly.

"Oh, yeah?" The young man slammed the bottle across the side of the bar.

We have all witnessed this exact scene in literally hundreds of movies and television shows. The bad guy snatches up a long-necked whiskey or beer bottle and bangs it against the top of the bar, where it shatters into a jagged weapon. The man had a right to expect dramatic results.

Apparently, however, bar tops were once sturdier, or bottles more fragile.

Two things happened as the redhead raised the bottle and slammed it into the bar. The beer in the bottle poured out all over his shirt and the front of his pants, and a chunk of the bar broke off, leaving the bottle unscathed.

He stood staring at the bottle in his hand with disbelief, then whacked it against the bar top again. It bounced harmlessly off.

"Ahhhhhhh!" He attacked the bar furiously, a scream of outrage escaping him. Perhaps a dozen times he slammed the unyielding bottle against the plastic and wooden top, doing a little damage but not hurting the bottle at all.

Finally, breathing hard, he stopped and stared at the beer bottle, a wet stain down the front of his pants. As a thin girl with bleached hair standing against the wall began to giggle, it spread down the line. Even the cop was smiling, although he still had his hand on the hard rubber grips of his pistol. The redhead's rage turned to embarrassment.

"Shit," he said, dropping the bottle. Then he turned, placed his hands on the bar, and assumed the position.

Coming late to police work as I did (just past thirty), I already knew I was not a Charles Atlas. In fact, being a realistic person, I had accepted many truths that elude most people throughout their lives.

I knew, for instance, by the time that I was sixteen that I was never going to be tall, dark, and handsome. The revelation came to me at a party where I was standing by many of my cohorts in the lobby of a theater. Catching a glance of myself amidst my friends, I was shocked to see that they were towering over me. It was something I had not realized. I adjusted my mental image to short, stocky, and rugged. I could live with that. Many women like men of that description.

By the time I was fourteen, I was also well aware that I was not an athlete. Years of being smashed in the face with baseballs and fumbling footballs at crucial moments had brought home to me that I was not graceful.

At eighteen, in the best physical condition of my life, my tongue would be hanging out after I had done a hundred yards of hard running. My drill instructor had to chase me for the last half mile of my required mile run in basic training, kicking me in the seat of the pants for the last quarter mile.

Physical things come hard for me. Even learning to use a handgun was a trial. I think maybe I always try to rationalize and intellectualize instead of simply doing it.

With all this self-knowledge available to me, I can fall victim to dramatic escapades. On occasion I still try to play the part set for me by television and the movies.

One such incident comes to mind.

"Ten–eighty-five, 10–85," the dispatcher intoned across the raspy airways. "Complainant says the next door neighbors are throwing beer cans into her yard and threatening her."

I grew angry as she gave me the address. It was an ongoing complaint. Two hoodlums had moved in next door to an elderly lady on my beat. Upon finding that she was afraid of them, they had set out to make her life miserable.

Virtually confined to her house by fear, she had called many times. The two hoodlums always managed to get inside before officers arrived. The woman was afraid to sign a warrant against them.

Gunning my car into her driveway that night, I was delighted to see that they were still outside in their back yard, just across a four-foot chain-link fence.

Several neighbors were out on their porches watching; I had an audience. Suddenly carried away by an adrenaline rush and a bad case of television cop syndrome, I measured the distance in my mind and decided that I could get across the fence and place myself between them and the door before they could get inside. It would require only a little acrobatic ability. In the heat of the moment, I forgot how small my acrobatic ability was.

Sprinting across the yard, carrying the weight of a metal flashlight, a two-way radio, pistol, PR–24 baton, ammunition, handcuffs, and leather, I hit the chain-link fence with my left hand, intending to use my momentum to vault over.

It almost worked.

Unfortunately, my PR–24 (a baton with a handle on it, derived from a karate weapon called a *tonka*) caught in the fence. It was a sickening moment. My entire body was in the air, my

117

legs higher than my head when the baton stopped my flight in midarc, then slammed me to the ground.

Lying on the dew-wet grass, the breath driven from me, I saw a back-up officer pull in and jump out of his car. He loped across the yard, vaulted effortlessly over the fence, and arrested the two drunken hoodlums who had stopped to watch the short, chunky officer make an ass of himself.

Yes, all the world *is* a stage. From time to time, however, all of us get to play the clown.

18

The Pills in the Golden Box

The rusty old Pontiac veered sharply across the center of the road as it swung for a right turn onto Clinton Highway. I had been watching for perhaps a quarter of a mile, suspecting from the slow, precise pace that the driver was drunk. The turn convinced me. I hit the blue light switch and bumped the siren once.

I had been cruising back and forth between Interstate 75 and Clinton Highway, waiting for the bars to close. It is ludicrous how the law works. As he cruises the highways, every cop knows that the people parked at bars and taverns are inside consuming an anesthetic, putting their brains to sleep. The law, however, does not allow an officer to use this knowledge as a reason for checking them *before* they drive. The officer must play a game, must follow long enough to witness something wrong, then hope they do not flee when he tries to stop them.

The old Pontiac wobbled to the curb and came to a lurching halt. Stepping from my cruiser, hand on weapon, I watched for movement in the car. Seeing none, I approached closely along the side of the vehicle, playing my light inside. A male driver and a female passenger were in the front seat.

"I need to see a driver's license," I said, standing back of the door post in case a weapon suddenly appeared in his hand.

119

"I ain' got it with me," he said. He was going to make me play games instead of just telling me right off that his license was revoked.

"Step out of the car and walk to the back," I said.

"Whas' wrong? What'd I do, off'ser?" He stepped from the vehicle staggering as he came, a medium built man of thirty or so with stringy blond hair and a blond beard. His clothes appeared to be expensive, in contrast to the beat-up old car.

"Put your hands on the back of the car. You're under arrest for driving without a license and driving under the influence."

"I gotta license, and I ain't drunk," he said belligerently. "Why'd you stop me anyway?"

"Put your hands on the car, now!"

He reluctantly leaned into the car placing his hands on the trunk. It was then that I made a mistake. I *assumed* that he was too drunk to fight, and assumptions can get you killed.

Instead of cuffing him first or at least kicking his legs into a severe position of strain, I bent to pat him down. I knew better. His elbow slammed into my face. A kaleidoscope of stars danced before my eyes as I was knocked backward. The pain of having your nose compressed is agonizing, and tears streamed down my face.

Fortunately, his intent was to escape, not to kill me. He sprinted off down a side road, amazingly fast for an intoxicated person. Rising to my feet in an indignant rage, I ran after him. Never had a prisoner escaped me after being taken into custody.

He had about a thirty-foot lead on me, which I was not closing. Drawing my baton, I paused and hurled it at him. In the movies, cops do this all the time. The baton slowly arcs ahead, catching the suspect behind the knees and bringing him gently to the ground.

My baton, however, turned end over end, striking him between the shoulder blades and knocking him forward to his hands and knees. I heard him grunt in pain. By the time I got to him, he was back on his feet.

I caught him by the back of the shirt, but my grip was tenuous. He swung his right arm backward, trying to strike me in the face again. I swung my large plastic flashlight at his head, and it shattered. But it did not stop him. As his shirt gave way with a ripping sound, I realized he was going to get away.

Turning, I saw the door of the old Pontiac open and sprinted back toward it, gasping for breath. The woman passenger was my key to catching the driver. She made it about twenty feet, staggering along, before I caught her by the arm.

"Whatta ya want with me. I ain't done nothin'."

"We'll start with public drunkenness," I gasped, trying to regain control of my breathing.

"Come on, gimme a break. You don't have to arrest me. You're just mad about him gettin' away."

"You're right on both counts," I answered. "It's my option to arrest on a misdemeanor. If I can identify your boyfriend, I may send you home in a cab."

"I don't even know his name," she whined. "He picked me up at a bar—tol' me he had some cocaine at home."

"So be it," I said, putting the handcuffs on her. "You're under arrest."

Records had run the car registration by the time I got to the jail. Now I knew who owned the car. When they found a picture of the owner from a previous arrest, I knew for sure who had smashed my face.

"I've changed my min'," the prisoner said. "I'll tell you his name."

"Too late. I know his name." I sat down at the booking table and began my arrest report. The woman—thin, with stringy, unwashed brown hair—propped her knees against the table. Her skirt fell away, revealing pink, lacy panties and causing several male prisoners to stand for a better look.

"Put your feet on the floor," I said.

She complied, wincing with pain.

"What's wrong?" I asked.

"Nothin'. Nothin' at all. Can't you reconsider about this? I wanna go home."

"Nope. I don't *un*arrest anybody."

"Baker 10," the dispatcher's voice rasped over the airways, "return to the jail and see the sergeant."

"I wonder what *he* wants," I asked Mike Upchurch. We were finishing up an early breakfast at the Waffle House.

"Who knows?" Upchurch drawled, reaching for his coffee cup.

In a few minutes I wheeled into the garage. When I got off the elevator, the sergeant was waiting.

"Did you search the prisoner's pocket book?" the sergeant asked.

"Of course, I did." My heart skipped a beat. Letting a weapon get into the jail can result in some serious time off. Then I saw the twinkle in his eye.

"And this box of valium was not in her purse?" He extended a gold box about two inches square by an inch deep. When he opened it, I saw that it was full of valium.

"Where was it hidden?" I asked.

"Ask the matron," he replied. This time he snickered openly.

The matron was sitting at the booking table. Beside her, the female prisoner stared sullenly ahead.

"She wanted to go to the bathroom," Connie said, her face blushing crimson. "When we got in there, she turned her back and fumbled around with her underwear. I caught her before she could flush it. It was wrapped in Kleenex. I had already strip-searched her, so I know it wasn't in her panties before. The tissue was wet. She had the box in her . . . you know."

"No wonder she kept trying to put her knees on the table," I said, whistling at the size of the box.

"Officer," the lawyer said, "my client is willing to plead guilty to public drunkenness if you'll drop the possession of a schedule drug for resale. She had a prescription for valium." He handed me a copy of the prescription.

"This prescription is six months old," I answered, handing it back. "No deal."

"What do you want then?" He was becoming irritated. "You'll never get a conviction for felony resale on just fifteen pills, especially when I produce the prescription."

"Tell you what," I smiled. "She'll plead guilty to public drunkenness, and we'll reduce the possession for resale to simple possession. The judge will probably go probation on that."

"That's ridiculous! We can beat it."

"Go right ahead. I've got the matron standing by. If your client wants the matron to get on the stand and tell the world the *size* and *location* of that golden box of pills, it's fine with me. Most women just carry them in their purse." This time I laughed out loud.

In a few minutes the lawyer returned, and the two of us went to the assistant attorney general, who okayed the agreement. The woman angrily paid her fines and left.

As for her boyfriend, the city police picked him up a few weeks later. He pleaded guilty to DUI fifth offense, driving on a revoked license, assault and battery, resisting arrest, and fleeing to avoid arrest. He got a year at the workhouse. Since I had placed a hold on his car, the five-dollars-a-day storage fee exceeded the value of the car by the time he was captured. It was sold for junk.

I heard rumors later that the girl got into a rehabilitation program, dried out, and married a car salesman. I would assume that any prescription medicine she uses these days is carried in a regular medicine bottle.

19

A Rose by Any Other Name

Most cops have a nickname. It may come about through fondness or dislike, or it may be the result of a single incident that (as Joseph Wambaugh said in *The Choirboys*) makes him a legend in his own time. Most nicknames come from other cops, some from the denizens of the highways and byways. Almost all are colorful.

My first police nickname was given to me by Lieutenant Jim Brackett who at the time was second in command on Baker shift. A stocky man of just about average height, with close cropped, sandy hair, and a perpetual mock-ferocious glare, he strode purposely everywhere he went. Brackett was a man's man and a total advocate of the officers under his command. He would fight like a mother lion when one of his troops was endangered.

He also had a wicked sense of humor and a quip for almost every occasion, which would be delivered with a deadpan expression. Early in my career, I was ranting and raving about how a suspect had lied to me.

"Why do you get so upset, Hunter? The man is merely exercising the skills of his trade to the best of his ability. He lies and steals *for a living*," Brackett said with a serious face.

As an officer who had come up through the Knox County Reserve, I had a lot of friends who still worked full-time jobs and did police work on weekends. Reserve officers love action, for the most part, and word got out early in my career that there was generally action in my vicinity. As a DUI enforcement officer, I was not tied to a beat but could answer "hot calls" all over the north. I arrested a lot of people.

One night as I was going in for the 10:00 P.M. to 6:00 A.M. shift, I found one of my former reserve mates waiting to ride with me. David Campbell and I were among the shortest officers at the sheriff's department, about five feet, six inches tall.

As we walked toward the squad room, replete with shining leather and polished brass, we met Jim Brackett. "Look," he said to whoever was with him, "the sheriff's department has organized its own Care Bear Squad."

He was referring, of course, to the little bears of cartoon lore who walked around with exotic symbols on their chests. The name stuck for years. Even today, some of my old Baker shift mates still call me "Bear."

The first part of the nickname, however, was dropped when a biker took a swing at me on Clinton Highway. Because my stick was in the car, I had to punch him out, something I rarely do because of potential damage to the hands. As we were hoisting him to his feet, one of my fellow officers commented, "The Care Bear has teeth." Thereafter, I was simply "Bear."

Mike Upchurch was christened the first time he got on the radio to make a traffic stop. A description of Mike's speech pattern is virtually impossible, one of those things you have to experience to understand.

The dialect spoken in East Tennessee is not what you think of as southern. While East Tennesseans say "Ya'll come back," just like other people south of the Mason-Dixon Line, the heart of the dialect is almost Elizabethan English, the result of isolation with only the King James Bible for literature.

The pronunciation of words with *e*, for instance, comes out almost as cockney English. An egg is an "aig," a leg is a "laig," and so forth. The vowels are distinctive, going something like this: "aih, aih, eye, oh, yew, and sometimes wi."

The *ing* sound is seldom pronounced in the pure Appalachian dialect. The *g* is usually dropped. Instead of running and jumping, the Appalachian tongue says "runnin' and jumpin'."

Television and radio have begun to homogenize most speech patterns in America, including the hills of East Tennessee. With Mike Upchurch, however, it never took. He speaks exactly the dialect he learned as a baby, without embarrassment. In addition, he speaks slowly and distinctly. His enemies (much to their chagrin) often make the mistake of thinking that his thoughts travel as slowly as his words.

Upchurch's first traffic stop went something like this: "Baiker Aighteen, I'll be tin-twenny-five with a grain Shivalay on twenny-five dubya at Baiver Creek Drive. Th' taig number is thray, aight, four, sevin, won. Thur'll bay thray white mails in the vaihicle." All this was delivered at the speed of a 45 RPM record played at 33 RPM. Translation: "I'll be 10–25 (in contact with) with a green Chevrolet on 25W at Beaver Creek Drive. The tag number is 3-8471. There will be three white males in the vehicle."

"My *God!*" exclaimed Mike Craig as he was about to have his first cup of coffee that evening. "If that country boy ever gets in pursuit, it'll be over before he gets it called in!"

The name stuck. Mike Upchurch thereafter was "Country Boy." He took it good naturedly and even bought a ball cap with the words of a Hank Williams, Jr., song on it: "A Country Boy Can Survive."

Pairs of officers can sometimes generate dual nicknames. One morning when Upchurch and I came in with eight or ten arrests between us, a sergeant commented, "The Clinton Highway Police department returns victorious." The name stuck and was later picked up by the newspapers.

Dispatchers, however, unhappy with the constant traffic stops from the two of us, dubbed us the "Dynamic Duo." "Batman and Robin can ruin a new dispatcher," one of them said. "They can literally drive you to distraction. They never slow down."

When my brother Larry joined the sheriff's department, it was noted that his style of police work was as aggressive as mine. We were quickly christened the "Brothers Grim," with someone commenting that sending both of us after the same subject would constitute cruel and unusual punishment.

At one point while I was on Baker shift, there were two extremely polite officers working side by side. After several trips to the same address for domestic disturbances, I told the captain one morning as the officers were checking in, "Captain, you better send me over there tonight. Those people are taking advantage of courtesy. It's like sending Wally and Beaver Cleaver after the Dalton Gang." That night there were arrests at the trailer park. I believe fear that the nickname would stick spurred the arrests.

The names *do* tend to hang on.

Ask Denver ("Denny") Scalf, a Knox County patrolman. Denny was unhappy because after many years on patrol he still had no nickname. He decided to take action on his own. Coming into roll call one night, Denny told us that he would thereafter answer only to the name of the "Big Kahuna," a character from the *Beach Party* movies of the sixties.

"Did you say 'The Big *Tuna*'?" Sergeant Robert Sexton asked.

A look of pain came over Denny's big, open face. He did not even try to protest. The laughter of his Baker shift mates told him that he had just acquired a new name.

He remained the "Big Tuna," or simply "Tuna," until he transferred off the shift.

When Jeff Palmer, then a rookie patrolman, failed to answer his radio one night, every available officer began driving over his beat looking for him. Every blue light was flashing in hope that he would see us and come to tell us what was going on.

Jeff is an unusual officer, noted for his courteous attitude and disdain for cursing. This is all the more unusual when you find out that he is an ex-Marine.

One night during Jeff's rookie year, he wheeled into the garage as I was leaving. As he angrily got out of his cruiser, I saw that he had a middle-aged, drunken female in the back of his car. She was yelling at the top of her lungs.

"I'm mad, Hunter!" Palmer said. A husky man of medium height with an almost perpetual grin, he was indeed a little flushed that night.

"What's the problem?" I asked.

"This . . . this, *woman* peed in my car—on purpose! She said if she could have gotten her pants down she would've done *number two!*"

"Oh no, Jeff," I said in mock horror, "not *number two.*"

"That's what she said," he answered, looking at her in disgust.

As we searched for Jeff in the early morning hours, all of us were becoming worried. It is policy to call in every traffic stop, but sometimes officers forget. Visions of Palmer in a pool of blood on some dark, isolated road were beginning to surface in my mind when another officer spotted him.

He had pulled into a vacant lot to catch up on his paperwork, unaware that he had forgotten to turn his radio back up after talking to a civilian. Jeff was embarrassed, as we all would be in such a situation. Unknown to him, however, he was about to receive a new name.

"Did you say Palmer was asleep when you found him?" someone asked as Jeff entered the service center office at shift's end.

"Yeah," the veteran patrolman said, "and it was such a *sweet* scene. I was afraid I'd wake him up when I took the teddy bear out from under his head."

When the laughter died down, Palmer had become "Cubby," sometimes shortened to "Cub." I am also grieved to report that Cubby's language has been corrupted through the years. There are times when he utters such horrible words as *damn* and *hell,* sometimes in front of other people.

Rookie Jim Pritchard acquired his nickname while doing a good deed one night. Every veteran knows that no good deed ever goes unpunished.

One night shift, he stopped in an area plagued by drunks to check two men parked in a vehicle. Both were drunk, and one fled on foot. There is nothing that will so quickly excite a good cop as a fleeing suspect. It is a reflex. The suspect runs; the cop chases.

Pritchard, however, stopped as the suspect plunged into the river and began swimming across. There *are* limits. One does not swim while wearing twenty-five pounds of equipment. He radioed other officers to pick up the suspect on the other side as officer Bill McKee arrived to back him up.

Midway across the river, the suspect started to run out of juice, and he began to flounder and yell for help. Pritchard and McKee located a canoe, but no paddles. They made their way out to the suspect, paddling with cupped hands.

The panicked suspect turned over the canoe as they were trying to pull him out, dumping both officers into the chilly waters. The rescue squad eventually retrieved all three of them. On the banks, Pritchard discovered that he had lost his portable radio.

Worst of all, the press (both newspapers) picked up the story.

It was a horrible day for Pritchard. Not only had he lost a piece of very expensive equipment, but he knew the entire shift would be eagerly waiting for roll call that evening at ten. They did not disappoint him.

As he entered the building, officers began to make strangling sounds and to yell, "Glub, glub, glub!"

Smiling good-naturedly (which is all he could do unless he *really* wanted to catch hell), he entered the roll call room where he was presented with a waterproof plastic bag attached to a long rope with a plastic float on the other end.

He was also given a new nickname. No longer would he be plain Jim Pritchard. Thereafter he would be "Jacques" Pritchard, in honor of the famous Frenchman, Jacques Cousteau, who pioneered the use of the Aqua-lung.

We could go on forever: Captain Bill Wilson, known affectionately as "Super-stump" because of his massive torso and short legs; Lynn McBee called "Fuzzy" because of his hair style; Jim Neubert, "Snail," because of his calm, slow way of doing things; Darrel Evans, called "Possum" because of his fascination with the creature of that name; and Jim Phillips, "Slugger," because it reflects his style of police work. You get the idea.

Women officers are not immune either. Janie Grigsby became "Calamity Jane" in a series of incidents that deserve a chapter of their own.

Colorful names for colorful men and women. It was the habit of some North American Indian tribes to rename members of the tribe when they reached a certain age or after a significant event.

Cops buy that practice.

20

The Cop and the Albatross

Cops will tell you right up front that they are not in the least superstitious. I agree with that myself. You take all the precautions you can, and there's nothing else you can do.

However, I never leave the house without my lucky key chain, my wedding ring, and my Saint Michael medallion. If I forget any of these, I am uncomfortable until I pick them up. It is seldom that I forget.

Saint Michael is the patron saint of cops or, to be more specific, warriors. Cops place themselves in this category. I am not Catholic. My brother (who is not Catholic, either) gave me the medallion because he was worried that I did not have one.

For years my brother Larry has worn a particularly beautiful medallion with Saint Michael the Archangel on the front and the inscription "Saint Michael Protect Us in Battle" on the back. When a shiftmate borrowed the medallion to have a duplicate made, Larry was injured the same day he lent it.

A few weeks later, the officer who had borrowed the medallion solemnly told me at a gathering of cops that it was his fault Larry had been injured. The officer had about four shots of Jack Daniels under his belt and was beginning to enunciate slowly, so I paid little attention to him.

Shortly afterward, my brother had the medallion dupli-

131

cated in gold for himself. He gave me the silver original and asked me to wear it. It has been with me ever since. I really do not believe it is anything but a pretty medallion, with no more power than my lucky key chain or wedding band, which also go everywhere with me. I am not a superstitious sailor, who believes in omens.

So let it be understood from the beginning that cops are not superstitious. When they begin to call another cop "Jonah" or talk about the albatross that is following him around, it is only a joke.

Harry Carrol is a tall, rangy man, who looks like he *ought* to be carrying a badge. In fact, he is a dead ringer for pictures of Pat Garrett, the western sheriff who killed Billy the Kid. A native Tennessean, Harry first became a cop in Texas, then moved back home.

Early in his street career at Knox County, Harry fell victim to an albatross. Mind you, no one really *believed* this, but his misfortunes strained the credibility of chance. Other officers joked about the invisible albatross, and some called him "Jonah," jokingly, of course.

Like most other officers at the Knox County Sheriff's Department, Harry did his time in the jail. After that he was transferred to the DUI enforcement unit and given a brand new Ford Cruiser.

The importance of a new cruiser cannot be overstated, especially when a department has "take home" cars as Knox County does. Officers are proud of their cars. Mostly, they take good care of them. When a department has "take home" vehicles, with one officer responsible, cars last four or five times longer than fleet cars.

A new cruiser is a status symbol. It is also a convenience, because the better car you have, the less down time you have, and the less time you spend driving one of the extra cars from the fleet.

Harry was naturally upset, as were his superiors, when he wrapped the brand new cruiser around a telephone pole a few days after he got it, totally demolishing it. These things happen, though, to everyone sometimes.

Cars cannot be replaced the way uniform shirts can be replaced. The replacement was an old Ford that sounded a lot like a farm tractor with a bad muffler. Harry was doomed to drive it, though, until a benevolent County Commission came up with more new cars.

Even without the car problem, unusual experiences always seemed to be happening to Harry. It seemed that he never arrested ordinary people. It was always those with lots of money, who always complained of one thing or another. At a business that had been hard hit by burglars, he drew down on a man thought to be a thief and put him on the ground, spreadeagled. He was a security guard. It was perfectly good police procedure, but not good public relations with an already irate businessman.

One early morning, though, something happened to Harry that was so outrageous, so far from the realm of random chance, that I began to look for the invisible albatross myself. It started with a drunk who did not want to stop for him. By the time the drunk did stop, Captain Bill Wilson and I were en route to back Harry up.

"Has he stopped an airplane?" Captain Wilson asked on the car-to-car channel as we topped the hill and Harry's cruiser came into sight.

It did look like an airplane parked on the highway. The light bouncing off our cruisers was blinding. As we approached, the reason became clear. One of the plastic blue light covers was missing from Harry's light bar.

We stood and looked at the light bar, with its missing cover. "I've seen them *knocked* off," the captain said, "but I never saw one just *fall* off."

"Hunter," there was a touch of anguish in the officer's voice. "I *know* it was on there when I started chasing him. The cover has to be somewhere between here and the city limits. Will you see if you can find it for me?"

"Sure, no problem," I said. It was only about a half-mile, so I expected no problem in finding it. After half an hour, though, I was beginning to have my doubts.

Up and down the highway I looked, first on the side he had been driving on, then the other. I was sure it would have been visible in the beams of my spotlight and takedown lights had it been along the road.

Finally, I gave up and started down the highway to give Harry the bad news. A pickup truck went by me, southbound, weaving from one lane to the other. I turned on my blue lights, and he fled. Just as I was about to call for back-up, the driver attempted a left hand turn across the highway. He missed the road completely and drove out into the middle of a field, where his truck came to a halt.

I ran out into the field and pulled the intoxicated driver out. As I put him against the car to cuff him, I saw Harry's blue-light cover. The front wheels of the truck—in the middle of a two-acre field—were perched on top of it. Needless to say, it was crushed beyond repair.

"Harry," I said over the car-to-car channel while wondering what the odds were against such a thing happening, "I've found your light cover. Do you want the good news or the bad news first?"

Eventually, the day came when Harry got a new cruiser again. He was out on the beat beaming at his good fortune when the brand new car overheated and shut down. The oil plug had been left out of the high performance engine.

It was not his fault, of course, so he got the car back, with oil this time. He was driving it the morning he yelled over the radio, "I've just been run off the road."

Arriving a few minutes later, Upchurch and I found Harry's cruiser perched on its tail against a steep embankment. A dejected Harry was standing by it. Fortunately neither Harry nor the cruiser was damaged.

Eventually Harry's luck improved until he was no more unfortunate than the rest of us. I always had a sneaking suspicion, though, that the albatross did not leave the vicinity.

There are some things that simply cannot be explained rationally. For instance, one night I stopped a car with no taillights on a lonely, deserted section of Highway 33 near the Union County line.

Upon stopping the car, I saw in the beams of my takedown lights that at least five shaggy people were in the battered old vehicle. Such situations make you think about your fragile mortality. I was several minutes from help, assuming that adjoining beat cars were not tied up.

Watching the car closely for movement, I opened my door. My flashlight clattered to the ground. As I reached to pick it up, my hand knocked it under the car. Standing for a moment, I thought things over. To get down on my knees would

134

mean having the suspects out of my sight, and there was no way I was going to approach a dark vehicle without good light.

An inspiration hit me. I would *back* my car up so I could reach the light. Never taking my eyes from the suspect vehicle, I put my cruiser in reverse and eased back. The sound of the flashlight crunching under the tire made a horrible sound.

With a deep sigh, I picked up my public address microphone and ordered the driver of the vehicle to leave. I am sure he was pleased as well as puzzled. He asked no questions, however, but drove away immediately.

How can you rationally explain what happened to a friend of mine several years ago? He was at a crossroads on a beat he had worked for years, he knew it like the tongue knows the inside of the mouth. He was a veteran officer.

After waiting for an hour for a suspect to leave a bar, he saw the individual come out, get into his car, and pull away. My friend gunned the engine and shot across the highway, right into the gorge that divided the two sides. Help arrived to find him still in the car, which was standing on its nose.

He told his supervisor that he had simply "forgotten" there was a gorge between the two sides of the highway. After all, he had only crossed at that point a few hundred times.

In 1984 one of the officers on my shift jumped a suspect in a stolen vehicle, and the suspect fled on foot. Rushing to his assistance, I spotted the subject as he darted across the road into an abandoned campground.

I was perfectly familiar with this old campground. I had worked security when it was open during the 1982 World's Fair. Poorly constructed, the roads running through it had begun to erode the first year. After two years of abandonment, there were gullies a foot wide and two and three feet deep.

Knowing all this, I gunned my vehicle onto the lot at full speed to cut off the suspect. The world became a slow-motion nightmare. The car soon became filled with flying clipboards, drawing tools, ammunition, flashlights, and all the vents from my dash as I hit the gullies without slowing down. It was like riding a two-ton bucking bronco. Worst of all, though, was when my head hit the roof of the vehicle, slamming my teeth together with a painful, jarring sound.

When everything settled on the floor and in the seats, I

could see the suspect climbing a fence at the edge of the inter-state. At that point, I had other worries. Fearfully, I climbed out of the car, expecting total devastation. With great relief, I saw that there was no damage. Walking to a nearby phone, I called for a wrecker so as not to be on the air with my misfor-tune. The driver snickered, but kept my secret. This is one reason why cops try to get along well with wrecker drivers.

One incident that happened at another agency (city to re-main unnamed) gave me a clear indication that we at the sher-iff's department do not have the only albatross in town.

It was a Saturday afternoon. A football game had just ended, and traffic was crawling bumper to bumper. It was so heavy, in fact, that traffic officers had been stationed at all major intersections to keep traffic moving.

At one intersection a motorcycle and car somehow ended up at the same point at the same time, and there was a colli-sion. Deciding that he probably would be blamed for the mis-hap, the officer directing traffic called for a photographer to record the scene. Details are a little hazy at this point, but essentially this is what happened.

The wrecker driver was standing by, waiting to clear the vehicles while the traffic officer directed traffic. The photog-rapher was leaning over the motorcycle, a cigarette in his mouth, focusing his camera.

Suddenly, and without warning, the motorcycle *and* the wrecker driver went up in flames. Bystanders quickly ex-tinguished the driver, who was only singed, but the motorcy-cle was a total loss.

As far as I know, that one is still being sorted out.

You do not have to be on the streets for bad luck to strike. It can happen anywhere. Ask the Knox County officer who was walking through the sheriff's department late one night, try-ing to unload a malfunctioning pistol, which he intended to have the armorer look at the next day.

The pistol accidentally discharged, putting a round through the wall of the sheriff's reception area. No one was inside at the time, but shooting holes in the sheriff's walls is still frowned upon.

Because there are mythical albatrosses and bad omens, it is always a good idea for a cop to maintain a little modesty. You never know when your words will come back to haunt you.

Back when I was a reserve patrolman, I asked a regular officer if I could ride with him one night. A stocky man with a walrus mustache, he put his hand on my shoulder and looked me directly in the eyes.

"Hunter," he said, "don't take any offense at what I am about to say. It's not personal. The fact is, though, I have too much time invested in my career to let amateurs ride with me. I can't take the chance that you might get hurt."

A few weeks later, he was on his way down to the jail when he stopped to check his weapon, a Colt .45, semiautomatic. It is carried in what is called "the cock and lock" position, with a round chambered and the safety on.

The control room operator, however, was an oldtimer with an inherent distrust of semiautomatic weapons. Despite the officer's arguments, the control room operator refused to touch the pistol until the hammer was lowered. In exasperation, the officer began to let the hammer down just as a reserve officer walked in behind him.

The pistol discharged, filling the small area with a horrible sound and the pungent odor of gunpowder. The .45 caliber slug hit the wall traveling at about 900 feet per second, then proceeded to bounce around inside the small enclosure. At one point it glanced off the lips and teeth of the reserve officer, cutting his lip and knocking him down. It had slowed sufficiently by that time, however, so as not to do any real damage.

I was one of many waiting for my chance with the arrogant officer. When the day came that he could no longer dodge me, I saw him flinch as I approached, smiling heartily.

"I just wanted to thank you," I said, "for the thoughtfulness you showed when I asked to ride with you. You were 100 percent right. Something *could* happen to a man riding in your car."

It just goes to show. If there really were such things as albatrosses or Jonahs, you never know when they might sit down beside you.

21

Tombstone Courage

An entire generation of youngsters watched Marshal Dillon walk out on the dusty streets of Dodge City every Saturday night. With a grim expression on his rugged face, he walked toward another man with a gun. Suddenly, both of them drew their pistols. There was the crack of two forty-fives and the bad guy went down.

Historians of the late nineteenth-century American West know that stand-up gunfights were the exception and not the rule. A real gunfighter went after his opponent with all the firepower (and usually stealth) that he could muster. The fatal shot was as likely as not delivered from a dark alley with a sawed-off shotgun.

The shoot-out at O.K. Corral (actually in front of Fly's photographic studio) between the three Earp brothers, accompanied by Doc Holliday, and their political adversaries, the Clantons and company, is often used as a classic example of an Old West gunfight between the good guys and the bad guys.

It was not typical at all, and you needed a program to tell the good guys from the bad guys. The shoot-out was the result of politics, plain and simple. Wyatt Earp was a candidate for county sheriff, and his brother Morgan was already a Tombstone city policeman. The election of Wyatt as sheriff, with Morgan already a city policeman, would have made things nice for the Earps, considering that Wyatt held a gambling concession at a downtown saloon.

As a deputy U.S. marshal, Wyatt had no jurisdiction at all in local matters. The only man on the Earp side with any legal standing at all was Morgan, the city policeman. The Earps, using the power of their respective offices, had conspired to run the Clantons and their employees out of town, eliminating adversaries who opposed Wyatt's run for the office of sheriff.

Just hours before, one of the Clanton group had been arrested and pistol-whipped by the Earps because his horse violated a city ordinance by stepping on the sidewalk. The Earps had decided to end the matter once and for all by shooting down the opposition or by making them totally lose face.

There is little doubt that the latter was what the Earps were expecting. The Clantons and their friends were ranchers, not professional gunfighters. They had shown great reluctance to take on the Earps, and there seemed little reason to believe that they would make a stand that day—if, in fact, it could be called that. One member of the Clanton group was not even armed when the Earps arrived.

Before the morning ended, there was a shoot-out with the reluctant cowboys. It was not, however, a stand-up, Hollywood-type gunfight, depending on the speed of the draw. Four professional gunfighters, none of them with pristine backgrounds, cut down the political opposition with superior firepower and skill.

The image-makers of Hollywood, however, could not sell tickets with the truth, so they cleaned up Wyatt Earp, just as they cleaned up Jesse James and Billy the Kid. In the cinematic versions, Wyatt faced the opposition, one on one, steely-eyed and righteous. That is the version young cops (and sometimes, not so young) remember and cherish.

When an officer is affected by this type of image, we say that he has "tombstone courage," because a tombstone is what it will get him. Officers under the influence of romantic television and cinematic heroes are dangers to themselves and others. They walk in on armed confrontations, weapons in holster, make unsafe approaches on traffic stops, and fail to take even the most elementary precautions. Strangely enough, women officers are just as prone to the disease as men.

One night I watched a female officer as she interrogated a burglary suspect on the street. She behaved in the best western hero tradition. When I pulled up, the suspect was backed against the car. The officer was standing nose to nose with him. She was on her toes to achieve the position, because he was several inches taller than she was and outweighed her by eighty or ninety pounds.

It was a dramatic episode. Watching, however, I was aware that the man could take her weapon or otherwise disable her with almost no effort. She was violating every safety regulation she had ever learned about keeping suspects at a safe distance and protecting the weapon.

She had convinced herself that no harm could come to "the good guys," that the blue suit would shield her from violence. Her intimidation of the suspect would have made a great television drama. In reality, though, such behavior holds the seeds of death. Through the years I have learned that there are many officers who share her misconceptions.

One Friday night I answered a domestic disturbance call in north Knox County. It was a miserable night. The rain was coming in sheets, and the ground had turned to soup. Entering a long muddy driveway, I found the complainant standing by the road.

She was a skinny, tired-looking woman of thirty or so. Clad only in a cotton tee shirt and panties, she stood by the driveway, arms crossed and shivering. The rain plastered the scanty clothing to her skin, giving the appearance of nudity. Blond hair hung in matted strands. Her right cheek bone was rapidly becoming purple.

"What's the problem?" I asked, getting out in the rain.

"He's beat me up for the last time. He just threatened me with a gun. I want to get my stuff and leave, but he won't let me back in the house. Just go with me, and I'll pick up my things!"

"What kind of gun does he have?" I asked.

"I don't know. It's little and black and square looking. Come on, I want my stuff, now!" For the first time I became aware of the strong odor of alcohol on her breath, and the red-rimmed eyes. She was drunk.

"Just a minute," I said quietly, "we need to talk. Do you have anywhere to go tonight—a friend or relative to take you in?"

"Yeah, but I ain't goin' without my clothes. It's your *duty* to go up there with me!"

"No, ma'am. It's my duty to resolve this situation without having anyone injured. Your husband is drunk and emotionally distraught. No one is in danger right now. You can pick up your stuff when he's sober—tomorrow. Tonight I'll take you to a safe place. I'd rather not shoot your husband or have him shoot me."

"You mean that the cops don't care if he beats me up? Well, I ain't goin' nowhere until you get my belongin's out of there!"

There was another alternative. The woman was drunk in a public place. It began to appear that I would have to arrest her for her own safety, and mine. Without warning, though, she forced my hand. Turning, she ran back toward the ramshackle house at the end of the driveway.

Cursing to myself, I notified the dispatcher what was going on and told the back-up unit to hurry. I had no choice but to go after her. Wading through the oozing red mud, I carefully watched the house as I approached. The woman was already inside. I heard my back-up pull in as I was about twenty feet from the house.

The door flew open, and a scrawny little man with disheveled hair and wild eyes stepped into the lighted doorway. His hand was behind him, at his hip pocket. "Hold it right there!" His words were slurred.

"Don't move or I'll shoot!" Standing in a crouch, holding the pistol in a double-handed grip, I centered in on his chest. The rain was running in rivulets down my face.

"Get away from my house. I ain't goin' to jail!" the man yelled. Beside him, out of sight, I could hear his wife screaming profanities at him.

"Bring your hand out slowly. If there's anything in it, I'll kill you. Let me see an empty hand. Now!"

Before the man could reply, the back-up officer walked past me, slipping and sliding in the mud, directly into my line of fire. "What's the problem, podnuh?" he asked in his best Wyatt Earp imitation.

I stood totally flabbergasted for a split second, knowing that if the man opened fire he would not only get the other officer, but probably me as well. I ran to a tree nearby and got behind it, covering the front porch with my Smith & Wesson revolver.

"She just pushed me too far," the man began to sob. "She never gets off my back."

"We'll take care of it, podnuh," my brother officer said. "We'll work something out!" He put his arm around the man's shoulder.

A few minutes later, I had the woman and her belongings in my car. I was smoldering with rage. In those days there was no domestic violence law, but today an arrest would have been mandated. At the time it was impossible. The man's pistol had been on the table behind him, not in his pocket.

As soon as we were alone, I turned my wrath on the officer, explaining that he was *never* under any circumstances to get between me and a suspect. He stood as if stunned at my rage.

"What's the problem? He didn't have the gun on him. It was on the table."

"You didn't know that! If he had opened fire, he would have killed you and maybe me because I couldn't return fire. You know better than that!"

"He's just a guy that had too much to drink and had a fight with his old lady. He didn't want to hurt anybody!"

"You didn't know that. He could have been off the deep end. When anybody makes threats with a weapon, *believe* them."

"Hunter, you'll have a nervous breakdown if you let this stuff bother you. Just don't think about it."

In amazement, I watched him drive away. Somehow he had survived for years without being killed or seriously injured. Maybe God does look after fools and drunks.

Training instructors know the statistics, and they try to impart them. Three out of four officers killed in the line of duty every year know, *before* arrival, that they will be facing an armed suspect. Still they die, many with their weapons holstered, often a few feet from cover that would have saved their lives.

A few years ago I went to back up an officer on "a man with a gun" call. The suspect had threatened neighbors with a double-barreled shotgun. At the time of the call, he was sitting on his front porch, cradling the shotgun in his lap.

Pulling in behind the primary officer, I racked a round in my shotgun, then got behind my cruiser to cover the man on the front porch. He was in his midfifties, wearing an old felt hat.

The primary officer, a man with less than a year on the street, got out of his vehicle, adjusting his hat. Then he walked toward the old man smiling like a miniature John Wayne. "How's it going today?"

Holding my breath, I watched, knowing that the man could kill the officer before I got off a shot. I saw the man's eyes dart toward me, then toward the other officer—calculating.

"Goin' all right. What are you doin' here? I never asked you to come."

Despite the hostile tone, the officer continued his stroll past several trees that would have made excellent cover. "Neighbors seem a little spooked about that shotgun of yours. You need to put it up."

"You can just get off my property. It's *my* shotgun."

Seconds later, the officer was so close that I could not have fired without fear of killing him. I breathed a sigh of relief as he snatched the weapon from the man's hands. He broke down the weapon and ejected two live rounds.

When it was over, I pointed out his error. The young officer smiled at me, the way your adolescent children smile at you when you try to teach them.

"I've been here before. The old man's harmless. He just wants to remind everyone that he's still somebody. Good police work is more than going by the book, Hunter."

I did not bother to tell him that the main objective of good police work is to be alive at the end of the shift.

They learn, though, if they do enough police work—and if they live long enough. The lesson is one that stays with them.

I once shared a beat with a young cop who had a bad case of "tombstone courage." He made every strategic error that could be made. He was a likable man but the most careless cop I ever worked with. "You worry too much, Hunter. Nobody's gonna kill you over a misdemeanor charge."

It was cold and snowing the night he learned his lesson. He stopped an old beat-up van because the taillights were out.

Taking the suspect back behind the van into the lights of the cruiser, he pointed out the violation. The man was unable to produce a driver's license, so the officer called records to check his status. He talked to the suspect in his laid back, good-old-boy manner while waiting for records to respond.

Without warning or provocation, the burly man snatched the officer's revolver and jammed it into his chest. Reacting instantly, the stunned officer caught the revolver across the top strap. With horror, he felt the cylinder moving in his hand, as the suspect attempted to pull the trigger.

A revolver, of course, will not fire unless the cylinder can turn. The only thing between the officer and eternity was his grip on the pistol. With a surge of adrenaline, he fought back, finally wresting the weapon away from the suspect.

He watched the man flee the scene, too winded to follow, then called for assistance. Two of us arrived within minutes. Seeing that the officer was not injured, we began a fruitless all-night search. The suspect was on home ground and was not captured until the next afternoon. Later, I talked to the officer.

"There was no reason for this," he said. "No felony warrants. Nothing serious. He was trying to kill me over a fifty dollar fine and a trip to jail."

"Welcome to the club," I told him.

"I don't understand. Why would a person commit murder over such a trivial offense?"

"You don't have to understand. You just have to believe that the next one is going to kill you. It won't matter *why*," I said. After that, he was one of the most cautious officers I ever worked with.

There are limits, of course, in a free society to what an officer can do. An officer cannot approach each traffic stop with weapon drawn, though it would be the safe thing to do. Police administrators answer to the public.

Officers could lead long, safe lives, though, even with minor restrictions. They continue to be their own worst enemies, especially in the South, where half the officers killed nationwide go down each year.

There are a few things *all* cops need to learn: (1) The shield is only symbolic and will not stop bullets; (2) Heroes in the movies get up, even after being fatally wounded, but real cops do not; (3) Wyatt Earp (or take your pick of heroes) was not what his legend proclaimed.

Any cop who can learn these few things, immensely increases the odds of survival.

22

It's Hard to Be a Monogamous Cop

"Did you, uh . . . call for an officer?" I asked. "Yes, and I appreciate that you got here so fast. I'll show you where I heard the noise."

The complainant turned and walked down the hall. She was a petite, dark-haired beauty, perhaps twenty-five years old. Full-breasted, with hips that flared into a heart shape, she was in excellent physical condition. I had no trouble at all ascertaining her physical condition because I could see everything but the soles of her feet. Her only item of clothing was a totally transparent jacket that only came to the waist.

"Right behind this door, officer. It leads into the garage. I heard something fall."

Stepping around her, I opened the door, reached in, and flipped on the light switch. Thankfully, there was no assailant waiting. I would have been his for the taking. My mind definitely was not on police work. It was in chaos.

This is the kind of call that cops kick around during slow hours. Almost everyone has such a story. It was the first time, however, that it had happened to me.

"Do you see anything?" She leaned into my bare arm and looked over my shoulder. The woman definitely was in good physical condition. There was not an ounce of fat on her.

"No, everything seems to be as it should," I said, stepping

away from her into the garage. "Well, I'll take a look around outside," I choked out through a dry mouth. It is difficult to appear casual when you are in the grip of raging hormones.

"It's silly of me," she said, "but when a woman has a husband who is on the road *weeks* at a time, she gets a little nervous." She stepped closer and removed a piece of lint from my shoulder.

"No, ma'am," I croaked out, swallowing hard. "That's why we're out there. Feel free to call any time you need us." I was edging down the hall toward the front door, expecting back-up to arrive any minute.

"Can I fix you a cup of coffee?" she asked, blocking my progress. "There's already some on the stove."

"That sounds very nice," I said, "but we are really busy tonight." We were not busy at all. That was why I was expecting a back-up unit, maybe a supervisor. If anyone else got a look at the woman, I would be in for a rough time. Few officers would believe I had declined such a blatant invitation. Even worse, they *would* believe it and begin to speculate. Either way, I would never hear the end of it.

"Oh well," the woman said, much to my relief showing no indignation, "maybe the next time. I *really* appreciate cops. Feel free to stop any night—if there's no brown van in the driveway."

I was standing at the bottom of the driveway, taking deep breaths when the back-up arrived.

"Everything all right?" the officer asked.

"Yeah, the woman just heard a noise in the garage."

"Are *you* all right?"

"Why?"

"You look like you just saw a ghost."

"Actually," I truthfully told him, "the complainant startled me when she first opened the door."

Every cop show has a hero who is divorced, is in the process of getting a divorce, or is separated from his wife because of the pressures of the job. The fact is, most cops go home to families like everyone else, though at odd times. Most are good husbands. Many of them coach little league ball and work with scout troops. The public image, though, is hard to shake.

The divorce rate *is* high, and extramarital affairs *do* contribute to the problem. I think, though, you will find the same thing to be true of bankers, lawyers, and clergymen. Infidelity is a major factor in many divorces.

It is my opinion, though, that most police marriages break up as the result of other related problems, the worst being an inability to leave the job at quitting time. Cops will tell you they never go off duty. They believe it passionately. The extramarital affairs, I think, begin to crop up in marriages already under other strains.

Cops see things on a daily basis that human beings ought not to have to see. They bottle it up inside themselves, refusing to confide it to their wives. After a while, they have to talk to someone; that someone is another cop. Many wives feel left out when their husbands gather to socialize. Presumably, it also works the same way for women cops, though I simply do not have the information to make such a judgment.

Before I ever hit the streets, I had a conversation that forewarned me of future difficulties. The person I was talking to was a jail matron who had been around cops for many years. The topic of discussion that evening had been a supervisor who had suddenly left his wife of twenty years for a much younger woman.

"You're married, aren't you?" she asked.

"Yes, I am."

"Have you decided which is more important, your marriage or your job?"

"I intend to have both."

"Oh, yeah? Well, what makes you think you're an exception? Divorce is the rule around here."

"Because I've been through one divorce, and I don't ever intend to go through another. I'm older than most of these recruits, and I know what I want. Besides, I have a strong marriage."

"We'll see how strong it is," she said. "You'll hit the road in that big police car with blue lights on top, carrying a gun and all that leather. Pretty soon the sweet young things will gather around you, telling you what a big, important man you are. You'll be having trouble with your wife because she'll hate the odd hours. Instead of pumping you up, she'll tell you to carry out the garbage. It won't be long until the sweet young things begin to look better and better. Finally, your wife will catch you, and there'll be one more divorce."

I did not know at the time that she was describing her own marriage, but I let the words sink in. Another divorce was not on my agenda.

The matron was right about one thing. Cops face more temptation than almost any other group of people I know. There are different categories of women to choose from, but the groupies cause the most problems. Every visible profession has its groupies. Those who follow the rock and roll stars, I suppose, are the most prominent, but every police department has them, too, no matter how large or how small.

A few years back, a television drama followed the career of a woman who stalked police officers. Every time she managed to seduce one, she would remove a bullet from his gunbelt, keeping them for trophies. The story was no exaggeration. Numerous women set out with the specific intent to have sexual contact with every officer in a given division or beat.

A motorcycle officer who is a close friend of mine told me a story about his first day on the job. He and another "motor man" were sitting astride their bikes passing the time when a sports car driven by an attractive young woman pulled up.

"Are you two members of the Blue Hawks?"

"Yes, ma'am, we are," the senior officer said.

"Well, that's good, because I've got a hankering to sleep with a big, bad motorcycle cop tonight and I haven't had either one of you." She gave them her address, then drove off, leaving the young officer in shock.

"I couldn't believe it," he said. "Of course, I was green. I didn't know that things like that happen to all cops."

One night in north Knox County I was breaking in a rookie who had never been in a police car before. At the beginning of the shift I had warned him not to expect too much because police work is generally routine and dull. The evening's events conspired, however, to make a liar out of me.

Ten minutes into the shift on the way out to the beat, a car in front of us hit the guard rail. The driver was extremely drunk and belligerent. At first he refused to exit his vehicle, then fought us when placed under arrest.

The rookie found himself in a fairly interesting fight his first ten minutes on the street. It was finally necessary to subdue the man with a nightstick. Two hours later, we hit Clinton Highway and began our bar checks.

It was around midnight when we walked into the first bar, a grubby little building of cinder block construction with the paint directly on the block. A flashing sign read: Nudes, Nudes, Nudes! I hardly looked twice, so calloused had I become to such things.

On a crudely built stage about two feet high, a totally naked woman was gyrating to a rock and roll song. The lighting was dim, except for the bright floods focused on the dancer. Other dancers lounged at the bar in various stages of undress, waiting their turn. It was obvious to me that the bar would not survive long. The competition was too great on Clinton Highway, and the cover charge was too high.

My rookie partner, a wiry man of twenty-five, craned his neck, taking in the sights. I let him watch for a few minutes, then started out just as the song ended.

"Officer," the dancer said, stepping down from the stage and carrying her costume in hand. She was blonde with a big chest and narrow hips, probably in her midtwenties.

"Yes?" I stopped as she approached. My new partner was caught against the wall by the door as the dancer pushed in close to speak to me. He could not move without touching bare flesh.

"You live in Northbrook Subdivision, don't you?" She looked at my name tag. "Officer Hunter?"

"Yes, I do." I waited curiously.

"I'm a neighbor of yours now. My husband and I rented a house down the road from you. I've seen you working in the front yard."

"Welcome to the neigborhood," I said for lack of anything else to say. From the corner of my eye, I could see the rookie. He was standing rigidly against the wall, Adam's apple bobbing up and down, trying not to stare at the naked woman inches from him. He appeared to be standing at attention.

"I have a lot of acquaintances who are cops," she said, then went on to name them. I knew I had a groupie on my hands and knew what she was going to suggest even before she did it.

"I'll be leaving here at two. If you want to see me behind the shopping center, we'll . . . ."

My partner had never heard such a suggestion, especially

151

not in such graphic language. I could almost *hear* his bobbing Adam's apple by that time.

When she had finished, I politely declined, thanking her for the offer. What she had suggested was not technically illegal unless charged for, but it was definitely in violation of general orders. She took the rejection good naturedly and told us it was a standing offer.

Outside, back in the cruiser, I acted as if nothing out of the ordinary had occurred. After a while, though, the rookie spoke.

"Hunter?"

"Yeah?"

"I'll be honest with you. I don't know if I can take too many of these dull and routine shifts."

Besides groupies and bored housewives, officers must contend with another source of temptation. It is to the benefit of bar owners for police officers to think kindly of them, especially the kind of bars found outside the city limits. There is no liquor by the drink there; these establishments are simply called "beer joints." They do not aspire to classy patrons. The nude bars are simply beer joints with entertainment.

In times past it was common practice for officers to partake of both the beer and the entertainment. The price was right. Bar owners wrote off free beer for cops as a business expense; those so inclined could partake of the dancers, also gratis.

Not all officers succumbed. Even those willing to crack down, however, were hindered by the fact that the owners had a mutual benefit arrangement with the people in charge at the time.

When Joe C. Fowler was elected sheriff in 1982, he put the word out that officers would be held to a higher standard than before. There was no general order forbidding officers to frequent taverns or nude bars, but it was understood that officers would thereafter behave decently. It took a while, but finally sank in. The bar owners spent a lot of money in 1986 trying to defeat Fowler, but it was wasted money.

Every police officer has his priorities. Drunk drivers were my first priority when I hit Clinton Highway in 1983. This was natural, since I was a DUI enforcement officer. According to the tavern owners, however, I was on a crusade.

I was only doing my job, but it *was* a nightmare for the bar owners. Patrol shifts rotate. At the most, an officer would be out for seven consecutive night shifts. Since some patrolmen are more lax than others, the bar owners did not have to contend with any single patrol officer more than a few days a month. They were stuck with me five nights a week.

It is hard on the bar business when patrons fear to drive home. They do not buy as much beer, and sometimes they even go to other places where they do not expect to be bothered. It was a proud night for me when the owner of one of Clinton Highway's roughest taverns stood shaking with rage and told me that I had ruined him, simply by rigidly enforcing the law.

The nude bars, however, still flourished. Their patrons drove from all over town, not just the local area. Still, I was a definite annoyance to them. Very cautiously, never leaving themselves open for a charge of bribery, they tried to corrupt me.

When I entered one of these establishments, I was always met with open arms by the owners and managers. They smiled even as I was snatching up drunken patrons. The first Christmas I was out, I found a case of expensive Scotch whiskey on the trunk of my cruiser as I was leaving one bar. Very carefully, I put it on the ground and drove away.

Another bar owner handed me an envelope with a pink ribbon that said "Merry Christmas, Officer David Hunter." He assured me that there was a friendly gift for every officer on the beat. I opened it and gave it back with a smile, telling him that five hundred dollars was just a little too extravagant and suggesting that he give it to charity.

Having failed to ply me with booze or money, one of the nude bar owners thought he had found my weak spot. I inadvertently brought it on myself.

A sign in front of this particular bar advertised beautiful women. In Knox County the classier nude bars have always been in the west end of town. The bigger, more expensive bars in the west could pick and choose dancers because there was more money to be made there. The north end bars got the girls who could not work in the west.

Some of these dancers were not what would be called traditional beauties. To the contrary, it was understood that a man *had* to drink a lot of beer in order to watch most of them dance

153

naked. Officers gave some of the dancers such nicknames as "Two Ton Tassie," "Lilly Munster," the "Stick Woman," the "Gourd," and "Twisted Sister."

One officer laughingly threatened to have the Better Business Bureau close down this particular bar for violating the truth in advertising law by boasting of beautiful women.

Walking through on a bar check one night and finding no drunks, I stopped to chat with the owner. As we were talking, a dancer climbed up on stage.

"She's new, isn't she?" I asked.

"Yeah, she just started a few nights ago."

"You'd better watch that. The next thing you know, these customers will be *expecting* beautiful women." I was joking, but she *was* beautiful. Still grinning, I left.

Two nights later I saw her for the second time. She was sitting beside the road in her car, a few hundred yards from the bar. As soon as I saw her, alarm bells went off. I drove by, calling another officer on the car-to-car channel, then went back.

She flashed a beautiful smile as I walked up. "I don't know what's wrong," she said. "It just died on me."

"Pull the hood latch," I said. Lifting the hood, I threw a beam of light in. Immediately I saw that the distributor wire had been disconnected. The door opened, and she walked up behind me.

"Do you see anything wrong?" Leaning over my shoulder, she pressed against me. The heavy odor of liquor mingled with perfume hit my nostrils.

"Yeah, I see the problem. There, it's fixed." I saw the cruiser coming toward us over the hill.

"That was quick," she said, stepping back unsteadily while flashing another beautiful smile. Looking at her flawless face, I once again wondered why the beautiful natural blonde was working the highway. I would later find she was a drug addict, banned from the more expensive bars.

"Why don't you follow me over to my room and let me thank you properly?" She stepped in closer, and I could tell that she was not wearing anything else under her light, silky blouse.

"Why don't you step back there to my cruiser? You're under arrest for public drunkenness. I should charge you with driving under the influence, but I didn't actually see you drive. Besides, I know who put you up to this."

She complied, seeming almost in shock. The other officer and I filled out a pull-in slip and called for a wrecker. Back in the cruiser, I saw her watching me in the rearview mirror as she sat handcuffed in the back.

"Are you gay?" she asked. There was no malice, only curiosity.

"No." I pulled away from the shoulder and started downtown.

"Then what's wrong with me?"

"Nothing. You're really beautiful. It just happens that I'm very much married to a woman I intend to live with until I die. Even if I wasn't, though, I don't like being set up."

She threw back her head and laughed. "Boy, did they figure this one wrong. They were overjoyed. The boss was sure he was going to bring you into the fold."

Through the years, until the dope finally reduced her to streetwalking, she was a valuable informant who brought me other informants. I was sad the last time I saw her being booked for prostitution. She had reduced herself to skin, bones, and hollow eyes.

The temptation is there for cops. It takes a strong will to walk away sometimes. Even had I been bent in that direction, though, I always remember what an old street cop said to me when I first hit the bricks.

"If you ever become sexually involved on the job, you destroy your effectiveness as a cop. You can't sleep with women and police them too."

Through the years I have had women with sparkling eyes ask me about the adventures and glamor of police work. I never burst a bubble by telling them that my idea of a successful shift is to go home alive, or that my idea of a really good day is to grill hamburgers with my family and friends, drink some coffee, and maybe later play a game of cards.

23

Warriors of the Twilight Zone

Every town has at least one. You will see them directing traffic or merely standing by the road waving be-
nevolently at passers-by. Sometimes they will be in full
uniform, sometimes they will be wearing only a tin badge
from the toy rack at K-Mart. Some are what a less enlightened
society once called "feeble minded," some are merely disturbed. All have one thing in common: they have become
what I call "Warriors of the Twilight Zone," individuals who
have convinced themselves that they are lawmen.

When I was a boy, there was such a man in the neighborhood. For years, every morning he would be at the bus
stop, flagging traffic around the bus. A small, shriveled man
wearing a cap pistol and toy badge, he was harmless enough.
All the children called him the "Sheriff." He would smile
broadly, showing a mouth full of gums totally devoid of teeth.

One evening the driver of a shiny Buick with New York tags
became lost, wandering down the back road where the
"Sheriff" practiced his trade. He pulled up to the "Sheriff"
and in his brash New York tone asked, "How do I get to Highway 25W, officer?"

All the children in the vicinity stopped to watch in amuse-
ment. They had seen the "Sheriff" give directions before. He
pulled off his cowboy hat with the peppermint stripe draw-
string and scratched his head.

"Wail," he said, "you go right down Mynatt Road, thataway, and turn left."

"Will that be 25W?" the man asked impatiently, chomping down on a cigar.

"Noooo, I reckon not. That'll still be Mynatt Road. It don't change, it just turns left. You gotta turn right then. You got anymore o'them seegars?"

"Sure," the man handed him a cigar, smiling a sophisticated smile. The "Sheriff" pulled it under his nose as he had seen it done on television. "So, when I turn right, will I be on 25W?"

"Nooo, that'll be Rifle Range Road."

"Will Rifle Range Road take me to 25W?" The New Yorker was fidgeting in his plush leather seat.

"Nooo, that'll take you to Dry Gap Pike." Showing a mouth full of pink gums, the "Sheriff" beamed at him.

"All right," the man was gritting his teeth. "Where *does* Dry Gap Pike take me?"

"Don't know. I ain't never been past Rifle Range Road."

"Sir, are you a police officer or not?" the irritated New Yorker asked.

"You see the badge, don'tcha?" the "Sheriff" said indignantly, "are you *ignernt*, or what? You sure do *talk* funny."

The Buick's driver screeched away, enraged, leaving ten or fifteen children laughing hysterically. No doubt the New Yorker went home with horror stories about hillbilly interbreeding and nepotism. We all enjoyed it immensely, reminding each other that gullible Yankees who went up to Gatlinburg and bought genuine Indian souvenirs, all of them clearly stamped "Made in Japan," could not be expected to tell the "Sheriff" from a normal person.

My first encounter with one of these individuals as a police officer came early in my street career. I was dispatched to west Knox County to work an accident involving a tractor trailer. Upon arrival, I found the truck on its side, a load of gravel spilled across one lane.

Cursing quietly to myself, I got out. It was hot, extremely hot. In minutes I was sweating, busily directing rush hour traffic near an intersection. All the traffic was coming west at that hour.

It was about thirty minutes later when I first saw him. He

was standing behind the truck, staring at the traffic and wearing a blue uniform with patches that said "Special Officer," the kind you buy at uniform shops. He was wearing a badge from the Knox County "Junior Deputy" program, a nightstick, and a walkie-talkie that looked to be of Korean War vintage. It had an antenna about six feet long.

My first impulse was to yell at him to get the hell away. I was afraid he would be hit by a car or that someone would use him as an excuse to run over me. Upon approach, though, I curbed my tongue. It would have been like yelling at a child.

His mouth hung perpetually open, and his eyes had a vacant stare. His teeth were so bad that most of his life must have been spent with a toothache.

"Officer," I said, "I have an assignment for you. Can you handle it?"

He nodded in amazement.

"Go back up the road there, to the next intersection, and slow the traffic down."

I watched him trudge away, then promptly forgot about him. It was a good three miles to the intersection, and I expected that he would lose interest and go on home. I still did not think about him when the traffic stopped. I was not familiar with the beat and merely thought rush hour had ended.

It was nearly two hours later when the truck was finally moved. By that time, I was drenched with sweat. My idea of heavenly nectar at that time was a big Coca-Cola from the first market I came to. No sooner than I had cleared from the call, however, the dispatcher gave me another.

"Baker 10, check a traffic jam. . . ." I listened in horror as she gave me the location of the intersection to which I had sent my helper. Arriving, I found traffic at a dead standstill—all the way to the interstate. He was standing firmly in the road, palm up, happily ignoring the angry, screaming drivers. It took me an hour to unsnarl things.

The incident left me wondering just how closely people actually *look* at a man with a badge.

Not all of the Twilight Zone Warriors are what we would call less than brilliant. One such man became an acquaintance while I was driving an ambulance in the late sixties. He was a psychologist who worked in a psychiatric ward.

He came by to administer a survey for a project, and soon he was riding around as an observer. It was on one of these "observation trips" that one of the drivers noticed he was exhibiting bizarre behavior. He was talking nonstop and making very little sense, and his eyes were bright, darting from side to side like frightened birds.

"The little freak's on bennies or RJS," Todd Chalmers said. Todd had never liked "college boys" in general, and liked Bobby Daniels less than most. Todd was good enough to explain to the rest of us that the pills he had described were "uppers" or "speed." There was not such a wide variety at that time, drugs not yet having become a national pastime.

Daniels eventually applied for a job but was turned down. By then everyone knew he was high almost all the time; people who work around doctors and hospitals generally have easier access to drugs than others. He stopped coming around, and I did not see him again until I went to an automobile accident in the county one night, several months later.

He was a well-groomed young man in his midtwenties, with dark hair worn short and slicked back. He looked neat in his Knox County Sheriff's Department uniform, which was gray at that time.

"How long have you been with the sheriff's department?" I asked.

"Just a little while," he replied, making notes on a clipboard.

I got busy and forgot about him. In fact, I did not think of him again until I heard Todd Chalmers talking to the ambulance service manager one evening.

"You remember that little pillhead, Daniels, who applied for a job here?"

"Yeah, I remember him," the manager said.

"I saw him last night. He's working for the Knoxville Police Department."

"Sheriff's department," I butted in.

"What?" Chalmers asked.

"I saw him at a wreck out in the county a couple of weeks ago. He was in a sheriff's department uniform."

"I don't care where *you* saw him. He came into the Krystal restaurant last night while I was getting coffee. He was wearing a Knoxville Police Department uniform. When he left, he got into a white, unmarked Plymouth with a blue light on the dash."

"Obviously one of us made a mistake," I said with a shrug.

Neither of us had made a mistake, though. In his quest for adventure, Daniels had applied not only for work at the ambulance service, but also with the city police, the sheriff's department, and the highway patrol. All of them had turned him down.

There are no solo ambulance crews, but cops often work alone. Daniels bought himself a blue light and a white four-door Plymouth, and went to work for *all three* local agencies. Through his employment at the hospital, he was able to steal citation books from all three agencies.

He apparently was a very polite officer. There were no complaints as long as he stuck to writing tickets in the traditional manner. Numerous people were convicted of traffic offenses written by him. Sometimes a judge would ask, "Is Officer Daniels here?" or "Does anyone know Officer Daniels?"

There were a lot of cops in Knox County, even then. Traffic cases are not contested very often, unless the officer angers someone, and apparently Daniels was a smooth talker. Eventually, however, he screwed up.

The uniforms were costing him a lot of money, so he decided to short-circuit the criminal justice system to repay himself. He began to fine out-of-state drivers on the spot. No one knows for sure how long this went on before the local cops were alerted that they had a pretender on their hands.

He was caught almost by accident. A supervisor with the highway patrol, so police lore says, drove by and saw an officer out of the car without his hat. This is a no-no with police supervisors, no matter what kind of uniform they wear. The highway patrol supervisor, of course, immediately realized that he had never seen Daniels before. Supposedly, though, he *looked* so authentic that the supervisor did a radio check to make sure he was not an out-of-county trooper.

The following story came to me from a retired Tennessee highway patrolman who was out on the highways in the wild and wooly days. He was in a two-man unit, many years ago, running in a county that borders Knox. Pulling into a small town, he and his partner saw that a new movie was playing at the local theater.

Having no portable walkie-talkies, the two of them were debating how to go in and watch the movie without getting caught. It was at that point that the local Warrior of the Twilight Zone walked by.

"He was a real polite fella," the old trooper told me, "not too bright, but nice. He always hung around cops. You know the kind. We'd give him old uniform shirts and used leather. He really didn't *look* too bad. Real neat, in fact.

"I called him over, and said, 'I got a job for you, trooper.' Well, he perked right up and came over grinnin'. I told him that me and my partner had to go inside on official business and that he was in charge of the car. I wrote down the unit number and told him to come right in and get us if the dispatcher called.

"I guess we had been in the theater watchin' a Jerry Lewis movie for about thirty minutes when I realized there was somebody standin' real close to me. I turned and saw it was the lieutenant, so I punched my partner and we followed him outside.

"'Lieutenant, I had somebody watchin' the car.' I was desperate enough to beg. This lieutenant was a real hardass.

"'I *know* you had somebody watchin' the car,' the lieutenant said. That was when I noticed that the lieutenant's shirt had a sleeve ripped out and that there was dirt all over his pants. 'I know about the guy watchin' the car, because when I saw your keys in the ignition, I went to get them out. When I opened the door, he *tackled* me and told me I was under arrest!'"

It was a long time before the trooper was again close to a town big enough to have a movie theater. There are some lonely places in East Tennessee.

Not even "professionals" are immune to the lore of police mythology and fantasizing when the opportunity presents itself. A few years back, a lawyer of my acquaintance was acting as a night magistrate, so his job put him in contact with cops on a regular basis. When this happens to any individual, one of two things happens: revulsion at the so-called police mentality or empathy. He fell victim to the latter.

From time to time he began to ride with me on the night

shift. We would have long conversations about philosophy and life in general. Once in a while, he would hint that he was dissatisfied with his professional life, and he would talk about how interesting police work is.

I would tell him that it really is not all *that* interesting, and only appeared to be because he never had to do any of the dull stuff, like writing reports or working accidents. Then something exciting would happen, and the cycle would start over.

"I'm armed," he said one evening while getting into the car. "Do you have a problem with that?"

"You're the judge," I shrugged. "You know the law."

"Well, it occurred to me that we might run into a bad situation and I'd be helpless." I only shrugged again. I had seen it coming and had hoped that no such occasion would ever arise. As much respect as I had for him as a lawyer, he was an unknown quantity as a gunfighter. Being squeezed between an assailant and an amateur gunman is a frightening situation.

There was no need for worry, however. He soon had an experience that dispelled all romantic notions about gunfighters and violence.

Walking into an all-night grocery store in the early morning hours, he got into line to buy a couple of items. As he stood in line, one of the employees leaned over from the side and whispered, "The guy at the front has a gun. He's robbing the store."

Suddenly things stood still for my friend. He became aware, as rookie policemen often do early in a career, that a pistol on the hip suddenly feels very heavy when it appears that you may have to actually use it. It is no longer an ornament or a badge of office. It is a tool of death and destruction, which may turn death and destruction in your direction.

He swallowed hard and stood there, thoughts running through his mind. The gunman had his back turned. It was an easy shot from five feet, but what if . . . the gun jammed? . . . the robber had an accomplice outside? . . . the gunman was wearing body armor? . . . the gunman returned fire before falling? Even worse, suppose it was a gag and not a real armed robbery?

These are all real concerns faced by cops each time a potential shooting situation arises. There is a difference, though, between even a rookie cop and a citizen with romantic ideas about gunfighting. The rookie has at least prepared himself emotionally and knows that violence may confront him at any time.

The only preparation my friend had received was hearing cop stories and watching television. These illusions vanished like fog in the sunlight when reality raised its ugly face.

Very wisely, he slipped out of the store, rushed to a phone, and notified the police of a robbery in progress. He was no longer troubled by the urge to enforce the law.

Every town has at least one Warrior of the Twilight Zone, at least one you can see. How many secret pretenders there are, we may never know.

Most little boys at one time or another dream of taming a town, of walking tall. In this day and time, a lot of little girls probably have the same dream.

24

The Other Country

We of mainstream America worry about whether our children will need braces, whether or not we will be able to trade cars this year, and if our latest raise will move us into a higher tax bracket. We drink beverages mixed by a bartender at the country club or in an establishment called a "lounge."

There is another America out there, though, another country altogether. In that America people worry about whether or not the food stamps will be cut this year, if a husband fresh out of jail will mean another "evaluation" trip to the welfare office, or if one of the children will be assaulted or end up in jail. That America drinks beer straight from he can, either in someone's living room or in a honky-tonk bar called a "beer joint."

The people of mainstream America are supporters of the Fraternal Order of Police, generally viewing officers as their protectors and friends. Their only negative contact with the law is an occasional traffic citation, more of an annoyance than anything else. Whether they realize it or not, they are grateful because cops maintain the status quo, the balance of power.

The citizens of that other America, divorced from the mainstream, do not become supporters of the police. Their contact with the police is much more frequent. People with money have marriage counselors and psychologists; the poor have cops. Whether they realize it or not, they resent cops for the same reason the affluent appreciate cops. Cops maintain the status quo.

If you have arrived at the American dream or if you are upwardly mobile, maintaining the balance of power is a desirable thing. If you are at the bottom of the heap, any change looks good.

Most citizens of this other America are not criminals. They work to raise decent children, who may climb out of poverty one day. Despite this, the view is different from the bottom. For instance, I once had a marijuana dealer rage at me as I transported him to jail.

"I would have been able to pay off my bills this week, if you hadn't busted me! I can't get out of the hole. Now, it's gonna take everything I made last week to make bond. You know I'm gonna be right back at it as soon as I get loose."

"Have you ever thought of getting into a legal business?" I asked. "Nobody would bother you for selling encyclopedias or insurance."

"Get real! I've got a tenth grade education. Nobody would trust me with their merchandise. The only thing I can raise is enough money to pay for my next shipment. If you people would leave me alone, I could run a profitable business and keep my family off welfare."

"Well, unfortunately, selling marijuana is against the law. You get busted every time we catch you. That's a fact."

"Yeah, and some of the richest people in America got that way by sellin' bootleg whiskey," he growled.

He had a point, so I merely shrugged.

Cops spend a lot of time in that other America. Many of them grew up in it. Officers tend to come from middle-class or working-class, conservative backgrounds. They believe in free enterprise, God, and the American dream. They believe in heroes and that good guys always win in the end.

Patrolling in middle America is pleasant. Officers often get out of their cars and chat with residents. Their children hang around and ask questions about the siren, the blue lights, and what kind of weapon you carry. Many of them tell you they want to be cops when they grow up.

When officers drive into that other America, however, the climate changes. You do not get out for a chat; anyone talking to a cop is likely to be called a "snitch." The children stare at you with hostile eyes. It is a policeman who puts Daddy in jail for being drunk on Saturday night. It is a deputy sheriff who stands by while the finance company repossesses the furniture. It is a deputy sheriff who comes with the hated Department of Human Services to take children into "protective custody."

Cops are the enemy in that other America. Get behind in your car payments and a cop comes with a paper. Try to hold a yard sale, and a cop comes to check serial numbers. If you have bought hot merchandise, they load *you* in a cruiser. You have a dispute with the landlord and refuse to pay until he makes repairs. What happens? A cop comes with the landlord to throw you out.

The first time a rookie discovers that other country, it is a rude awakening.

Three of us walked into the bar on a routine check a few weeks after I went on patrol. It was a place I had been warned not to enter alone. The advice had been previously ignored, though. In my rookie mind I could not conceive that anyone would dare to intervene in a legal arrest. A drunk might fight back, but other patrons would never assist him.

I had no way of knowing how lucky I had been up to that point.

"That one by the pool table looks too young to be in here," I said.

"Yeah, and pretty well drunk, too," another officer added.

Threading our way through the crowd of a hundred or so, we surrounded the young man. He was short and chunky, with ragged blond hair and watery blue eyes.

"I need you to step over to the door so I can talk to you," I told him.

"Why?" He was surly.

"Because you look underage, and you look drunk. Let's move, *now*."

He put down the pool cue and turned as if to comply. Without warning, he threw a back kick as artful as any I have ever seen in a martial arts display. His heel struck me just below the rib cage, driving the wind out of me. I managed to get a grip on his shirt as I went down.

The world became a flurry of action as I gasped for breath.

167

My two companions had gotten a grip on the struggling man and were moving toward the door. When the first thump hit the side of my head, I was shocked. Then feet and hands began to rain on us as we fought our way to the door. A furious crowd had turned on us.

It felt as though we were moving through molasses as we inched our way to the door. Eventually, however, we fought our way through, and one of the officers began swinging his baton, holding the crowd back. It had been impossible to draw the batons in the closeness of the packed bodies. Finally, someone locked the door from the other side.

Sitting in the hospital emergency room an hour or so later, I was being taped into a tight bandage. The cartilage had separated from the bone where it joins the rib cage. I never knew if the initial kick did it or if someone scored from the sidelines.

"What happened?" the emergency room doctor asked, pulling the tape tightly and painfully into place.

"I just learned a valuable lesson," I replied.

"And what might that be?"

"I just found out that not everyone looks up to cops."

"I would have thought that you already knew that," the young doctor said.

"Knowing on an intellectual level and knowing in your gut are two different things," I replied.

"Well, you definitely know it in your gut now." He tapped me lightly on the taped ribs.

There are points, however, where both Americas overlap, where they have things in common. You do not run into them very often, but when you do, the memory stays with you.

From day one of my patrol career I had been known as an implacable foe of the taverns and honky-tonks up and down the highways. It was understood that I did not tolerate drunk and disorderly conduct on my beat. Establishments that could or would not keep order found me spending a lot of time there. If underage drinkers slipped by, the establishments stood to lose their license. Some bars had not survived.

Mike Upchurch and I jailed more than one thousand people on a two-mile stretch of highway during a three and one-half-year period. The denizens of the highway knew us well, either from firsthand experience or because we had jailed a friend or relative. To say that I was unpopular among the bar patrons would be a vast understatement.

"Baker 10, can you meet me at the market?" The caller was a rookie DUI enforcement officer.

I pulled in a few minutes later to meet with him. Technically, I was not his superior, but a smart rookie learns from the survivors.

"A guy just pulled in here and told me there's an infant in the back of an old blue car over there. He says the baby has been in the car for about an hour and that it's crying."

"Come on, let's check it out." It was cold out that night, not yet full winter but too cold for an infant to be without heat.

In minutes we had located the baby in the back of an old rattle-trap car. Seething with rage, I opened the door with a metal "slim jim." I picked up the baby and patted it. The skin was cool to the touch. I handed the baby to the rookie officer.

"I'll be back in just a minute." I strode to the door of the bar, determined to find the owner of the car if I had to check identification on the seventy or eighty people inside. I was aware that I needed more back-up but was not at all inclined to wait. I expected no assistance from anyone inside.

"I need the guy who left the baby in the car," I said to the doorman, a man I had jailed more than once.

"It's the big guy in the flannel shirt. The one with the beard." I looked at the doorman, shocked at his assistance. "I'm the one who sent the guy after the cop, Hunter. There's some things you just *don't* do."

"Are you the man who left a baby outside in a blue car?" I asked as I approached.

"What if I am? It's *my* baby and *my* car." He was a big, heavy man in his midtwenties with a sneer on his pocked face.

"You're under arrest for child abuse by neglect. Walk out that door and put your hands on the side of the car."

"Piss off," the man said, leaning over the pool table for another shot. "I'll raise my kid any way I want."

Catching a handful of greasy hair, I slung him toward the door, not caring if the world was watching. He turned, an expression of shock on his face, as if he intended to resist.

"Fight back," I said. "Give me an excuse."

"No way." He put his hands behind his back and walked outside to be cuffed.

Huddling with the other officers, I explained the procedure for taking a child into protective custody. As we were leaving, I turned to the rookie.

"I'll have twenty complaints tomorrow that I brutalized this poor man by pulling his hair."

"I don't think so," the officer said, looking over my shoulder. It was then that I heard the clapping. It was soft at first, then louder.

Turning, I saw fifty or sixty bar patrons, many who had ridden to jail in the back of my cruiser. They were applauding what had happened. I stood stunned for a moment, not quite grasping the situation. Finally, I raised my hand awkwardly and waved before climbing into my cruiser.

"Officer Hunter," the burly doorman said, "you need any witnesses, you know where to find 'em."

"Thanks," I said.

It would be an exaggeration to say that the incident that night changed my attitude or the attitudes of the bar patrons. It was a point of contact, however. We had crossed the boundaries of the two Americas. We had found something about which we agreed.

For a brief moment we were able to see each other as human beings. I was not merely the cop on the beat looking for an arrest, and they were not merely potential problems.

We were all just people concerned about a little child.

25

Never the Twain
Shall Meet

"**O**ffisuh Hunter, can I ast you a question?"

I paused on the backwalk of the Knox County jail, where I was assigned in 1981. The man who had assailed me was a black inmate who had just pled guilty to murder. He was holding a newspaper, a puzzled expression on his face.

"What do you need?" I asked.

"The newspapah say I pleaded guilty to murder and was sentenced to life."

"That's what it says. I read it this morning."

"This is wrong," he said. "I never pleaded guilty to no murder."

I stopped, intrigued by the direction in which the conversation was going.

"Elliot, in order to have pled guilty, you had to have had this explained to you at least twice, once by your lawyer and once by the judge. The judge won't take a plea bargain unless you convince him you understand it. You took the life sentence to avoid the death penalty."

"Man, they was talkin' a lot of shit. I don't unner'stand half of it. My lawyer, he just said goin' along wit' him would keep me outta the chair. Ain't no way they could convict me of murder."

"Elliot, are you saying that you didn't rob the old wino, then kick him to death because he only had a little money?"

"Sho' I done it," he answered. "Ol' man was worthless."

"Then why do you say there was no way you could have been convicted?"

"Because nobody *seen* it. If nobody seen it, then it never happened. How could they convict me?"

That conversation had a lasting impression on me. Every sociologist and psychologist who deals with criminals should work in a jail for a while. The traditional philosophy is that any criminal can be rehabilitated if enough therapy is administered.

Let us examine this concept for a moment.

Therapy is the treatment of a disease or illness, administered to make an individual well. It follows, then, that therapy only works if an individual is ill. If I go out tomorrow and begin to shoplift, therapy is in order. I will have become ill. For me, shoplifting is an abnormality, requiring treatment.

To a professional shoplifter living in a criminal culture, however, theft is not an aberration and cannot be treated as such. The abnormality in a professional shoplifter would be *not* to steal. His wife might ask, "What's wrong with you? You ain't stole nothin' all week. The kids are gonna starve if you don't get out and earn some money."

More simply put, true criminals do not share with mainline society a system of ethics. They go through an entirely different thought process. Criminals do not perceive themselves as wrong. They perceive mainline society as being wrong.

"Don't do the crime if you can't do the time." This is a cornerstone in the society of professional criminals. It means that jail is an occupational hazard of their way of life. To a member of mainline society, the thought of being locked up is terrifying. To a professional criminal, being locked up is a time to renew old acquaintances and to plan new crimes.

I have known a certain criminal for about twenty years. I will call him Jimmy. We met long before I became a cop and before he was ever caught and jailed the first time.

Jimmy was the youngest of three brothers. It is a fact that he grew up in a rough environment. So did his two brothers, who went on to become successful members of mainline society, and hundreds of his peers who shared his environment. His mother doted on him, and he never lacked love or a stable family unit.

I first met Jimmy when he was assigned as my partner in 1969 when I was driving an ambulance for a living. It was the first civilian job he ever had. During the sometimes long hours between calls, he would boast about the five thousand dollars he squirreled away while in the U.S. Army overseas, selling goods on the Korean black market. I passed it off as a youthful indiscretion.

When my brother caught him stealing from the dead, it began to dawn on me that perhaps the problem went a little deeper.

"I don't understand what you're so upset about," Jimmy told my brother, who had confronted him in rage and disgust. "He was dead. The money won't do him any good."

"Because he's been at the morgue for twelve hours and because he has a family that has been looking for him," my brother raged.

"Hell, he was an *old man*," Jimmy said. "Nobody lives forever."

It was eleven years later when I saw him again. He was awaiting trial on three counts of aggravated assault following a shoot-out with a narcotics officer. He had already done two terms in the state penitentiary for various criminal activities.

"Hello, Jimmy."

"What's goin' on, Dave? You just come to work here?" His hair was shot with gray. There were deep lines in his face.

"I didn't think you were here when I caught my last time." There was no embarrassment at being behind bars. It was his professional environment, freely entered.

"I read in the papers what happened. It looks like you might catch some heavy time," I said.

"Naw, I'll walk on this one," he said. "When the jury hears what happened, they'll cut me loose." I looked at him in amazement. He was not a kid, not a romantic, as I recalled.

"How do you figure that, Jimmy?"

"I only fired in self-defense," he said, lighting a cigarette.

"The paper said they were stopping you because they had good information that you were transporting morphine. Is that not true?"

"Yeah, but you don't know the whole story."

"I'd like to hear it. I have a few minutes."

"Well, to start with, they violated my constitutional rights. There was nothin' wrong with my drivin' or my car when they tried to stop me. That's why I wouldn't stop. Cops can't just pull somebody over without a reason."

I did not interject that the Supreme Court considered probable cause based on a reliable informant a perfectly good reason to stop a car. I was fascinated with his logic.

"The only reason I fired the first shot was to give'm fair warnin' that I wasn't gonna give up. That's when they opened fire on me. After that, I didn't have a choice. It was self-defense. That's when I started firin' my sawed-off shotgun at them. They were tryin' to kill me."

"And you think a jury will cut you loose?"

"Yeah, I do. Besides that, the cops fired a lot more rounds than they admitted. I got witnesses to confirm that."

"Well, good luck, Jimmy."

"Thanks, Dave."

Before the case got to court, his lawyer had convinced him that the self-defense ploy would not work. His lawyer worked out a deal where two counts of aggravated assault would be dropped in exchange for a guilty plea on the morphine possession and one aggravated assault. He had a separate indictment on each of the three shots he had fired, plus the narcotics charge.

This would have put his time in the thirty-year range. He turned down the deal and pled guilty to all three charges of aggravated assault in return for the dropping of the narcotics charge. He was sentenced to twenty-five years on each of the aggravated assaults. I was aghast when I found out about the deal he had turned down.

"Why?" I asked.

"Well, you ain't ever been a convict so you probably won't understand that there are different kinds of time. There's hard, and there's easy. With a narcotics conviction, they'd never let me be a trustee. As it is, I can get my old job back as barber. I got connections. I used to cut the warden's hair. He likes me. It'll be easy time."

"Yes, Jimmy, but it's seventy-five years of time!"

"I knew you wouldn't understand, and I can't explain it. I

ain't ever asked you a favor before. If you got any clout, though, help me get moved to the walls as soon as you can so I can get established again."

He was right, I did not understand. By that time, though, I had already figured out that a criminal's mind does not work the way the mind of a noncriminal works.

The convoluted thinking was never clearer to me than during a conversation I overheard at a holding tank one night when the prisoners did not know I was listening. It was a conversation between a professional cigarette thief and a "new buddy" who had just caught his first prison term.

"I'll tell you one thing," the new buddy said, "they may kill me, but they'll never rape me."

"Shit boy, you don't know what you're talkin' 'bout." I heard the cigarette thief pause to light a cigarette. "You're gonna get raped. Ain't no ifs, ands, or buts about it. You got no friends at the walls. If you fight back, you'll be dead and raped. It's your *initiation*, boy. It's a occupational hazard. You be a stand-up guy, though, make some friends, get somethin' goin' to make money, and you'll be rapin' other people pretty soon."

There was a chorus of agreement from other convicts in the tank. I shuddered at the reality of that other universe, the existence of which I had no doubt.

The underworld, if you want to call it that, has its own logic. To mainline society it is perverted and sick. It is there, though, with its laws and codes of behavior.

For the most part, social workers and sociologists do not believe in this other society. There are two good reasons. The main reason is that no convict will ever speak a word of truth to an outsider. I think it may be emotionally impossible for them. Second, social workers start out with an answer in mind, then look for a question to fit it.

Noncriminals sometimes commit criminal acts. You can save those people from "a life of crime." Just as likely, they will save themselves if they survive the process. Anyone can make a mistake. The system, however, is set up to keep those people out of the penitentiary. Today, a first offense is unlikely to send anyone to jail for more than a short time.

Criminals know this. Most of them manage to keep having

"first offenses" for a long time. The last time, he was put on probation. Charges were dropped after probation, so his next crime will again be a "first offense." Lawyers' fees are the income tax of a professional criminal; prisons are their universities.

Very early in my career, it was my job to oversee kitchen trustees. A career criminal named Ray took me under his wing. "I like you," he said, "so I'm gonna give you two pieces of valuable advice that'll stay with you forever. First, never threaten a convict. Do what you wanna do. They won't like it, but they'll know that you know the rules. Convicts see threats as weakness. Second, *never* trust *any* convict."

Ray was a master cook. Every morning he made a "test run" of gravy and biscuits. This enabled kitchen guards to eat early, although they were supposed to wait until after the prisoners had eaten.

"Hunter, I need to borrow twenty dollars," he said one morning. "It's my mother's birthday next week. I ain't seen her in eight years, and she's gettin' old. I know it's against the rules for you to loan money to prisoners, but I ain't gonna tell anybody. One thing for sure, I ain't goin' nowhere," he laughed.

How can you turn down a man who teaches you great truths and feeds you superb breakfasts? I lent him the money.

Two days later, I went to work and found that Ray was gone. There was a new cook.

"Where's Ray?" I asked.

"They shipped him to Brushy Mountain," one of the other trustees answered.

"That was kind of sudden, wasn't it?" I asked.

"Nope, he knew he was goin' a week ago," the trustee said.

When I came in for work the following evening, an afternoon shift officer stopped me. "Hunter, that convict cook asked me to give you this, before we shipped him to Brushy. I know I'm bending the rules a little, but I used to see you talking to him all the time."

"Thanks," I said. Back in the office, I opened Ray's note. It said: "Dear Officer Hunter, Always remember them two things I told you, and you'll never git took again. Best wishes, Ray."

I sat down and had a good laugh at myself. It was as close as I ever came to actually *communicating* with the other side.

Career criminals put great faith in the system to work the way it is supposed to work. One night I listened to an enraged drug dealer ranting and raving after returning from a preliminary hearing, where he had been bound over to the grand jury. His outrage was not so much at being caught, but because, in his opinion, the officers had broken the rules. I cannot testify, one way or another, as to who was telling the truth, the dealer or the narcotics officers.

According to the dealer, he had been outwitting a particular officer for some time and thoroughly enjoying it. This is his story.

"I'm sittin' on the couch watchin' television when the doorbell rings. I've got seven hundred 'ludes in the bedroom, but I ain't worried, even when I see the cop outside. I know he's got no probable cause to come in.

"So I open the door. The cop pushes his way in and two other cops follow him. When I try to stop him, he hits me with the shotgun. They search my apartment, find my dope, and charge me with possession for resale and resisting arrest.

"I still ain't worried. I know it's an illegal search and arrest that'll be thrown out at the hearing. I couldn't believe it. That cop got up there and *lied*. He said that a friend sent him over and that I *let* him in to buy some dope. I don't mind bein' caught fair and square, but he *lied* on me."

"For the sake of argument," I said, "suppose he did lie. You've already told me you were selling drugs. Don't you think it ought to count for something that you're guilty?"

"Hell no! You're missin' the whole point. This is a country of laws. If the cops don't stick to the law, how the hell are we supposed to stay in business? I couldn't turn a profit if the cops came every time they knew I was dealin'. I'm dealin' all the time! By God, it's not right for cops to break the rules! The whole system could come apart."

Kipling wrote: "East is east, and west is west, and never the twain shall meet." You can say the same thing about career criminals and mainline society.

26

The Bad Seed

Psychologists and sociologists have been debating for some time as to whether environment or heredity is the major factor in the development of a human being. Those who hold with the theory of heredity say that the genes will win out, no matter what kind of environment you put an individual in. The other side of the debate says that environment is almost all-important.

Those who believe that environment shapes individuals tend to blame all crime on society. To borrow an analogy from science fiction author Robert Heinlein, these people believe that you can take a horse, send him to school, dress him up, and he will become something other than a horse.

Country folks have another way of saying what Heinlein said. It goes like this: "Trying to teach a pig to sing is pointless. It will frustrate you and only annoy the pig."

Being the pragmatic people that they are, cops accept a little of both theories, but swallow neither whole. Every day of their lives they go into environments that are unspeakably vile. There they find good and decent people raising healthy children.

They also go into houses of luxury and find selfish, whining people raising selfish, whining children. Cops know that good neighborhoods can produce bad children and bad neighborhoods can produce good children.

Cops tend to look very closely at parents when deciding

179

whether to lock up a juvenile or send him home. A strong, loving parent can raise decent children under almost any circumstances. Weak, gutless parents can mess up a kid, no matter what other advantages he has.

From time to time, however, cops run upon situations that leave them totally perplexed. They can find no explanation for someone's behavior. It is at that point that you hear cops use an unscientific term: bad seed. They are referring to children raised by decent, hard-working people living in a good neighborhood who are absolutely incorrigible from childhood up.

A few years ago I answered a fight call in a modest middle-class suburban subdivision. It was an unusual situation in such an environment of church-going, conservative people.

Upon arrival, I found a man in his late thirties, neatly dressed and well groomed, administering a thorough, efficient thrashing to a young man of twenty or so. I immediately recognized the young man on the receiving end of the whipping. He had often come to visit his brother when I was a jailer. His brother was awaiting trial for his second rape and was eventually convicted. At the time of the fight, he was serving time.

"All right," I waded in and pushed them apart, "knock it off!" I sent the enraged man across the street and the one being thrashed into the yard of the house where the fight had occurred, warning him not to leave or go inside. Another man bore a strong family resemblance; I later learned that he was a third brother.

"What happened?" I asked the enraged man after a back-up unit had arrived.

"My wife was out for her evening walk. Those two were standing in the yard by the car. The one I was fighting with yelled at my wife and asked her . . ." he looked around at his neighbor, suddenly embarrassed. "He offered her ten dollars to have sex with him."

I accepted his sanitized version of what had really been said and called his name and birthdate into records. As I had expected, he was clean, without so much as a traffic citation. Leaving him, I went across the street.

"I want that man arrested. He come up here and started beatin' me for no reason at all!" the young man complained. He was lanky, with uncombed hair and had a tooth missing in front.

"That's right, officer. I seen it," the second man said.

"Both of you give me some identification," I said quietly.

"Why?" the first man asked. "I ain't done nothin'."

"You were involved in a public brawl, and I smell alcohol on your breath. Now give me some identification. Don't give me any more lip."

For the sake of this story, I am going to call these men by the name of Crowder, offering advance apologies to all the Crowders in the world. I have never to my knowledge had dealings with anyone called Crowder, but chose the name at random.

In a few minutes records came back with a criminal history on both individuals. The second brother—not involved in the fight—had done time for rape, as well as for disorderly conduct and public drunkenness several times. The brother involved in the fight had a long history of drunken violence. I would learn later from officers familiar with him that he, too, had been accused of rape, but no substantial case had ever been put together on him. Rape, it seemed, was a recreational activity among the three brothers.

"You gonna arrest him for beatin' up on me, or not?" Fred Crowder asked.

"Yeah, how about it?" Lawrence Crowder chimed in.

With my own eyes, I had seen the gentleman thoroughly wear Fred Crowder out. There had been no weapons involved, however, so the charge would be simple assault, a misdemeanor in Tennessee. Officers have broad discretion on most misdemeanors. I decided to hold "curbstone court." Curbstone court is a proceeding held at the curb by cops. It is probably the most widespread legal proceeding in America.

"So you want me to arrest that man for assaulting you. Is that right, Fred?"

"That's right!" For the first time I noticed his eyes. It was like looking into the eyes of a lizard. There was life and movement, but no hint of humanity. He had the feral, crafty look of a fox crossing the road with a rabbit between its jaws.

"Well, I'll try to be fair, Fred. If you insist that I arrest him, I will. Of course, I'll also have to arrest you for disorderly conduct and public drunkenness."

"What'd I do?" He was pretending indignity.

"He says you offered his wife fifty dollars to go to bed with you."

"That's a joke. I only offered her ten." He looked at his brother and snickered. Almost immediately, he realized what he had said. "I was only jokin', though."

Stepping very close, so as to keep the conversation private, I talked to both of them. "If that had been *my* wife, you probably wouldn't have been able to walk away from here. Both of you are going to get in that car and leave. Neither of you will ever come back to this neighborhood again. Understand? I would love to throw you in jail, but I don't want to lock up the gentleman across the street!"

They dropped their heads and went to their car without a word. In a few minues, they were out of sight.

"Officer," said an attractive middle-aged woman who was standing by the road wringing her hands, "they drove my daughter home from a party. It was in a nice neighborhood. I'm sorry about this."

"Ma'am, I have two things to say about that. You and your daughter are both lucky to come out of this unharmed. And you don't owe me an apology. You owe it to your neighbors."

A year or so later, I cruised by a closed market on my beat. An old car was in the parking lot, engine running. A woman was behind the wheel. Easing onto the lot, I got out of my cruiser. Before I could speak to the woman, Fred Crowder walked from behind the building out of the darkness.

He stopped and looked directly at me, then began running clumsily across the parking lot. Having every reason to suspect a burglary, I sprinted after him. I caught up with him in the middle of the highway and grabbed him by the collar.

Turning, he swung a right hand at my head. Blocking it and stepping inside, I hit him along the jawline with my open palm, hard enough to stagger him but not to render him unconscious. He charged back again. Sidestepping, I drove my fist into his solar plexus and let him collapse, holding his left arm, on which I immediately snapped the cuff.

"Why did you chase me?" he gasped.

"Why did you run?"

"Because I knew you'd put me in jail for bein' drunk," he grunted.

"You're a perceptive man, Fred. If you didn't break into

that store, the only charges will be public drunkenness, assault on an officer, and resisting arrest." I hauled him to his feet.

"I ain't a thief," he said indignantly.

"Definitely not your family specialty, is it Fred?"

"You're just arrestin' me because my name's Crowder!"

"No, Fred, I'm arresting you for public order crimes. The fact that your name is Crowder is just icing on the cake, a bonus for a job well done, a little personal satisfaction!"

After ascertaining that there had been no break-in and finding that his wife was sober, I sent her on her way. Back in the car, I satisfied my curiosity.

"What were you doing on this lot at this time of morning, Fred?"

"Takin' a leak."

"*Why* were you here?"

"I had been dancin' with my girlfriend. She dropped me off, and I called my wife to come after me."

"Does your wife know about your girlfriend?"

"Yeah, why?"

"She doesn't object to your having other women?"

"What difference would it make? She's just another slut. They all are. If she don't like it, she can leave."

A chill went up my spine, not because of what he was saying but because of the way he was saying it. He was talking about women as if they were not human. I began to ponder the matter of two convicted rapists in one family. When the opportunity arose, I spoke to the mother who had raised the vipers. I was expecting Lucrezia Borgia.

"Mrs. Crowder, I'm Officer Hunter. Could I speak to you, please?"

She was a small woman, well groomed, with neatly styled hair. Even at past fifty, a prominent dimple in her chin gave the impression of a young girl.

"Certainly." She had just watched as my testimony sent her son to jail. It was not a long sentence, but confinement nonetheless. Hostility on her part would have been understandable.

"This is absolutely none of my business, but . . ."

"You want to know what made my boys the way they are. I wish I could tell you. Fred is the only one of the three who hasn't been to prison, but not for lack of trying. I'm sure he'll eventually make it. Could we sit down?" We took a seat in the lobby outside the courtroom.

"Mrs. Crowder, does your husband . . . Has your husband made a practice of . . ."

"The first thing the school psychologists asked about was violence in the home. In thirty years my husband has never hit me. There's no family violence and no broken home to blame the situation on. John, my youngest, threw a puppy into a bonfire when he was six, then laughed about it.

"Once, when they were all between eight and twelve years old, they broke into a neighbor's chicken lot and killed every chicken by knocking their heads off with a broomstick. There has never been any remorse from any of them, no matter what they did.

"Lawrence and Fred molested a nine-year-old girl when they were twelve and ten. She wasn't seriously injured, so the parents didn't push it. That was the last attack we knew about until they sent Lawrence to prison the first time. John, as you probably know, is there now for rape." There were tears in her eyes by that time.

"I appreciate your time, Mrs. Crowder."

"It didn't help much, did it, officer? You were expecting me to be some kind of monster, and I understand. They defy any kind of explanation."

She may have lied to me, of course, but I don't think so. I have been in their house. The father is a quiet, seemingly mild man who seems as puzzled as everybody else. The house had no *feel* of violence about it, and cops learn to recognize the symptoms. The only charge to be leveled is that they should have put all the boys out on the street long ago.

Unfortunately, the Crowders are not unique. Any cop can point to more than one situation in which seemingly decent people raise monsters and where neither heredity nor environment explains what has happened. Maybe some day the learned mechanics of the mind will be able to tell us why such things happen.

Until they do, though, cops will tell you that there is no way to account for the bad seed.

27

"He Didn't Mean No Harm"

There are some things a policeman understands: robbery, lies, even the slaughter of another human being in a drunken rage. The policeman does not condone these things, but he understands how they come to be.

A person who harms a child, however, is beyond the scope of his understanding. When a cop goes after an armed felon, he goes prepared. Before he is finished, the felon may be dead or the officer may be dead. It is a part of the job.

The armed robber or the burglar has a reason for the things he does that a cop can grasp. In his own warped way, a thief is making a living. You arrest him without much emotion most of the time because he is a thief and you are a cop.

A child molester stuns even a man or woman hardened to suicides that leave bone fragments and brains on the wall. It shames a cop to be a human being at times. Still, the cop does his job because it is his job.

"I have a warrant for aggravated rape," the homicide detective said. "Anybody here know Johnny Swazey?"

Mike Upchurch and I both raised our hands. 'Who'd he rape this time?" Mike asked.

"A nine-year-old girl. He lives with the mother. The rape took place this afternoon while the mother was at work."

"It's a change anyway," I said. "He raped an elderly woman the last time, then stole her pocketbook. What's he doing back on the streets? It hasn't been five years since he raped the old lady."

"Copped some kind of plea bargain, I guess. I need a couple of officers to go with me and pick him up," the detective said. "The little girl's still at the hospital. We want to pick him up before the mother takes the child home."

"Hunter and Upchurch," the captain said, "and I'll go."

In a few minutes, we pulled up in front of the residence. It was a shabby place on a back country road. Upchurch moved around to cover the back without being told. The door was not locked.

We walked through the trailer, looking in closets and under beds. No one was there. We were about to leave when I saw the toy baby bed in the living room. A lifelike doll was tucked in, as if a little girl had put it to bed.

Rage swept over me. A child, a little girl, *had* put the doll to bed. It was perhaps the last time she had done so with the total innocence of childhood. She would certainly not ever be the same again. They could patch her up, but they could not return her to her original condition.

"The mother says there's a shed out back where he spends a lot of time," the detective said.

We walked across the yard to a green metal shed. I was praying that he would be there; I very much wanted to see him. We found only an old musty couch and a table in front of it. The table had a huge ashtray filled with cigarette butts and cumpled cigarette packs.

"He doesn't work," the detective said. "I wonder how he supports his habits."

"He probably steals," I said. "Come on, let's go to his parents' house."

"Nobody's dumb enough to go home after what he's done," the detective said.

"He'll go home," I said. "He's a crybaby and a mama's boy. His mother was there every visiting day when he was in jail. She dotes on him. He's probably already there."

A few minutes later, we were on the front porch of his parents' home. It was a nice, middle-class ranch-style house. I knew his father was a hard-working man.

"We have warrants for Johnny, Mr. Swazey." I said when he opened the front door. The look on his face was one of extreme sorrow. He stepped out on the porch.

"He's not here, officer. I know you have to look. He *was* here, but my wife took him to the preacher's house."

"No need to search the house if you say he's not here," I said, "but you know we have to pick him up."

"She'll bring him back. How's that little girl?"

"As well as can be expected, I guess," the detective answered. "We need to take him in now, Mr. Swazey."

The phone rang as the detective was speaking. Mr. Swazey stepped inside the door and answered it. Emotion played over his face as he listened, then spoke. "The officers are here now. Bring him home!"

"She's bringin' him home now. She listens to the preacher." We all walked down to the end of the driveway to wait. The man seemed to want to talk.

"When they arrested him over the older woman, I didn't believe it. I did everything I could for him. But the little girl wouldn't lie. It's hard to believe your son is a . . ." His voice trailed off.

A half hour later, Mrs. Swazey still had not brought him home.

"Captain, there's no use in hanging around here. I have some things to check," I said.

"I'll call if he shows up," the man told us. He walked tiredly up the driveway.

A few minutes later, I had found one of my best informants. I got out my notebook. "I want every place you know where I might find Johnny Swazey—hangouts, relatives, friends."

The informant knew Swazey well and gave me a fairly long list. I went hunting. I did not intend to let Swazey enjoy another night of freedom. By 2:00 A.M., however, I had exhausted my leads. I drove past the trailer where the search had started, thinking he might have returned. There was a light on, so I stopped.

A dark-haired woman looked suspiciously out the door before opening it. "I'm Officer Hunter. I saw the light and thought I'd check on you."

"We're all right. Have you caught him yet?"

For the first time I saw the little girl, hanging to her

mother's skirt. She was tiny, delicate looking. Her eyes were two black pools of terror. I wondered how long they would look that way. I started to pat her on the head, but she recoiled from me. I swallowed hard.

"No, we haven't. We will, though. I *swear* it." Walking back to the car, I felt tears of rage brimming around my eyes. I sat behind the wheel, breathing hard until I regained control. The little girl's eyes were one more horror in a long line of horrible things I had seen in my life, things I knew I would never forget.

I roared northward on the interstate vowing that I would keep his parents' house staked out until he showed up or was captured. Before I arrived, however, I heard the homicide detective on the air. He had staked out the house after we left, and the suspect had surrendered without a struggle.

The homicide detective slowed and stopped as we met down the road from Swazey's house. Swazey sat, head down, refusing to return my stare. It always amazes me that human monsters do not have some characteristic to warn the rest of us of their twisted, perverted nature.

"His mother saw us in front of the house earlier and turned into a driveway. She had the idea that some cop might want to hurt her baby," the detective said.

"I can't imagine why she would think that," I replied.

Later, in a calmer frame of mind, I was glad things had worked out the way they had that night.

Unfortunately, the little girl was not through with Swazey.

"You saw *what?*" I asked in disbelief.

"Swazey's girlfriend was here today. She brought the little girl in to see Swazey," the jailer said. Knowing that I had been involved in the case, he had brought me the information. "I was standin' right next to his booth. Swazey asked her how the car was doin'. It was like a regular family visit. I thought you'd want to know."

Later that afternoon I drove past the house where the little girl had been raped. There was an old car in the driveway. I had seen it earlier, parked in front of the Swazey house.

In Tennessee, felony cases first go before a sessions court judge who conducts a probable cause hearing. If probable cause is found, the case goes before a grand jury. The grand jury finds "true" or "not true." If true, the suspect is indicted and the case goes to criminal court for trial. Swazey was waiting for the grand jury to hear his case. Without the little girl's testimony, the grand jury would have no choice but to let him walk.

Three or four days later, I fell in behind the mother's "new" car and saw that she had no brake lights. I pulled her over and approached with the citation book. The little girl was not with her. "You have no brake lights. I need to see your operator's license."

She got out of the car and handed me the license, then stood looking at me as I wrote the ticket.

"You were out there the night my little girl was . . . the night of the incident."

"I was there the night your little girl was pinned to the bed by a two-hundred pound man and forcibly penetrated. The word is *rape*." I went on writing the citation.

"Well, things are not always as bad as they seem. Johnny's really a good person. I've talked to his therapist, and she says he couldn't help himself. You can't send a sick person to jail."

I started to tell her you could find a therapist to plead Hitler's case on the grounds of childhood deprivation, but I did not. My control was slipping as I stood there, remembering the twin pools of terror that were the little girl's eyes.

"I know you don't understand, but my little girl does. He didn't mean no harm. I explained to her how people sometimes do things they don't mean when . . ."

"Sign right here," I interrupted. "This is not an admission of guilt. If you fail to show, however, a warrant will be issued for your arrest. I'd suggest you get those lights fixed. I'm out here almost every day."

She signed the citation as I stood and stared at her the way I would stare at a worm I had found in my food. She handed the pen back, and I looked her directly in the eyes. A woman in her late twenties with a splotchy complexion and watery eyes, she flinched under my gaze.

"You don't have any right to judge me!" she shouted at my back. "And you don't have any right to judge Johnny."

You should thank God that cops don't judge, lady, I thought. *Just thank God for that.*

I was not privy to the case, but when it was over I learned

that the woman had tried to interfere. She had tried to prevent the little girl from testifying. Under threat of being prosecuted for child abuse by neglect, she produced the child when ordered, however.

"That little girl testified like a trooper," the investigator said with a smile, "no thanks to her mother. Swazey can think about this for the next forty years."

Forty years seems like a long time, but I have faith that the court system will find a way to get him back on the streets while he is still young enough to rape someone else.

In 1981 I booked a man who had just raped an eight-year-old girl. In early 1988 I saw on a printout that he had been paroled. Within months we had him in jail for raping a twelve-year-old boy. I do not believe for a moment that these are the only two children he has destroyed.

Social workers wring their hands and say there is no solution to the "problem" of child rapists. There most certainly *is* a solution, at least after we catch them the first time.

Ask any policeman what it is.

28

"Two Beers Is All I Had"

In November 1982 I came back from the Tennessee Police Academy proudly wearing a shiny new badge and the uniform of a certified Knox County officer. I was proud. Most officers at the sheriff's department begin their careers as jailers at Knox County. It is the proving grounds.

Being a jailer is a horrible job. The abuse piled on jailers is unbelievable. Everything from verbal assaults to having urine hurled on you is part of the job. I was the best jailer I could be because I was raised to earn my paycheck, but I was glad that my time would come to an end there.

Many patrolmen at Knox County quickly forget how it was, and they begin to treat jailers as second class officers, forgetting that the arrest is often the easy part. I made up my mind never to forget what I had endured and what the present jailers are enduring. The jail was a crucible: I walked out a better man.

There was no hesitation, though, when a job bid was posted. I submitted a bid. At the interview, I was handed a surprise. "This job will be as a DUI enforcement officer. Do you still want it?"

Until then, DUI (Driving Under the Influence) enforcement officers had worked out of the Criminal Identification division, but the sheriff had just transferred them to patrol. They would continue, however, to work the same schedule.

At the time, all DUI enforcement officers worked straight

nights, Tuesday through Saturday, 10:00 P.M. to 6:00 A.M. Patrol officers worked (and still do) swing shifts. A patrolman at least had the occasional weekend with the family.

Last but not least, the DUI enforcement officers were looked upon by regular patrol officers as something a little less than a street cop, even though they took the same risks as everyone else. It was not a glamor job.

"Yes, sir, I still want the job." I did not hesitate, though several officers said they would wait for a "regular patrol job." I wanted to be on the streets, to do what I was trained to do. The night shifts were fine with me because I have always been a night person. As for the opinion of the patrol officers, I intended to change that.

In a few days I had my cruiser and other equipment. The officer assigned to train me, Henry Wood, was amused at my gung ho attitude. He assured me it would pass, though it never did. I still do police work the way I did then, although I now work in a different area.

For two weeks I rode with Henry, learning the basics. Finally, my night came.

"Do you see how the cars in this lane of traffic are backed up?" Henry asked.

"Yeah." I was driving Henry's cruiser, nervously trying to remember where all the switches were.

"That usually means a drunk driver. People are afraid to pass them because they weave back and forth. Pull into the outside lane and move up."

In a few minutes I had worked my way to the front of the line. Sure enough, an old Oldsmobile was wobbling back and forth across the white line.

"No doubt about that one," I said, reaching for the blue light switch and accidentally turning on the siren, which was at full volume. Henry quickly adjusted the switch.

"Sir, step out of the car," I nervously said.

"Wha's wrong?" the man asked, his head bobbing loosely at the end of a long neck and his eyes moving erratically in their sockets. I was assaulted by the smell of his alcoholic breath. Henry stood back watching.

"I believe you're driving under the influence of an alcoholic beverage. Now step out of the car."

The man opened the door and stood up swaying, holding to

the car for support. "I only had two beers all night, off'cer." It was the first of hundreds of times that I would hear the phrase "I only had two beers."

"Stand away from the car, there on level ground. I'm going to give you a field sobriety test."

"I'll get the pull-in slip," Henry said, walking away. There was obviously no doubt about the man's condition, but the tests have to be conducted or a lawyer will hang you out in court.

"All right. Put your feet together." The man complied, swaying like a tree in a windstorm. "Close your eyes and extend your arms like this." The man complied. "Now lean backward as far as you can."

At that moment a carload of teenagers went by. They leaned out and yelled at me, as they nearly always do when they pass an officer who cannot chase them down. I glanced at the car, annoyed but aware there was nothing I could do about it.

I turned just in time to see my prisoner going down, arms straight out, eyes closed, a serene expression on his face. He did not collapse, but fell like a tree, doing exactly as I had told him. He slammed into the ground so hard that I feared Henry had heard him fall. He was still busy with the paperwork, however, not looking.

Hurriedly, I ran to the man and lifted him up. He was breathing regularly but was out cold. I propped him against the side of the car.

"What happened?" Henry asked.

"He just passed out," I replied, thankful that he had not seen the incident and that my prisoner had not damaged himself. I had just learned a valuable lesson, all by myself: never take your eyes off a drunken prisoner.

After the weeks of training, I was assigned to north Knox County, where I would spend most of my street career. When I first went out, there were six bars on a five-mile stretch of Clinton Highway (25W) in the county alone. There were others scattered at random over the rest of the north. Clinton Highway, however, was where the action was.

It was early February 1983 when I embarked on my career as a police officer, running north. During the next few years, reporters would refer to me and Mike Upchurch, who worked with me, as the "Clinton Highway Police Department."

The police academy teaches the basics, but the streets are where a cop is baptized by fire. I set out to do what I had been assigned to do, which was to arrest drunk drivers. I went at it with passion, as I do everything in my life, whether I am writing a book or changing a set of spark plugs. Life is too short to waste time not enjoying yourself.

No matter how serious an officer is about his work, however, he must maintain a sense of humor. Police work is a profession that quickly kills you if you do not learn to laugh.

"All right," Lieutenant Norman Cawood said to the obviously intoxicated complainant, "what's the problem?"

Norman Cawood is a tough street cop with sense of humor sparkling just below his mock-ferocious glare. Well respected by his subordinates, he never lets things get him down. I have never seen him at a loss for words.

"I gave the girl a hundred dollar bill," the man was swaying as he talked. "She brought me a beer and change for a ten."

"Is that true?" Cawood asked the manager.

"I don't think so, but I can't keep up with every transaction," the manager answered with a shrug.

The incident in progress was at a nude bar. Music blared. The place was packed with weekend revelers.

"That ain't all," the complainant said, belligerently.

"So, what else happened?" Cawood asked.

"The next beer I ordered, she done the same thing."

Cawood stared at the swaying man for a moment. "Let me get this straight. You gave the waitress a hundred dollars, she brought you change for ten. Then you gave her *another* hundred-dollar bill?"

"Right. She kept that one too," he said with righteous indignation.

"How much have you had to drink?" Cawood asked.

"Just two beers," the man said, falling against a car.

"Turn around," Cawood said, "and put your hands behind your back. You're under arrest for public drunkenness. I'm saving you ninety dollars. You can thank me later."

"You're makin' a big mistake," the man said from the back seat of my cruiser. "You take *me* to jail, and I'll have you walkin' a beat downtown."

"Is that right?" He was a big man, in his late thirties and wearing a loud polyester suit. He had given an automobile dealership as his place of employment, just after blowing .21 percent on the Intoximeter. "How did you plan on doing that? I work for the sheriff's department. We don't have any walking beats."

"*Sher'ff's* Department? Where am I, anyway?"

"On Clinton Highway, near Anderson County." I was waiting for a wrecker, passing the time.

"I knew this was a trick," he said, falling sideways then sitting up abruptly.

"How's that?" I asked.

"I never drink in the county. This is a set-up if I ever saw one. My wife's behind it, right?"

"I don't know where you did your drinking tonight, but this is where you got arrested."

"Oh, yeah?" he leaned forward, attempting to focus his eyes through the plastic screen. "Then just tell me why you stopped me. You gotta have a reason to stop a man."

"Well, I always get suspicious when I see a man driving up a dark highway with no lights on. When he has grass and flowers hanging from underneath the car, I really get suspicious. Between me and you, though, driving off into the ditch for no apparent reason is a dead giveaway."

"Oh, yeah," he leaned forward again, his head wobbling. "Besides that, why did you stop me? I only had two beers all night."

The wrecker came then, and I got out of the car. The wrecker driver looked at the man's vehicle and whistled softly. "That's a beauty," he said. "It's a shame it belongs to somebody who's gonna wreck it one night."

"Yeah, it looks like a new one. You don't see many Studebakers in that condition today." I handed him the pull-in slip, and he signed for the car.

"Where are you takin' me?" the prisoner asked as I got back in the cruiser.

"To jail," I replied, pulling away.

"You'd better not. Me and Sheriff Van Riper is like brothers."

"That might help if we were in another county, but Joe Fowler is sheriff in Knox County. He wants me to arrest drunk drivers." I went to the next parking lot and turned around. As we drove back down the highway, the wrecker pulled away, towing the man's car.

"I'll be damned," the man said, looking out the window of the cruiser.

"What?" I asked.

"That wrecker is towin' a '57 Studebaker. I got one just like it. I didn't think there was another one in the county like mine. Even the same color."

"It's a small world," I told him.

A man or a woman may have an I.Q. in the genius range but, when drunk, they behave the same as their less-well-equipped peers. One example is a ploy tried so often that it is like waving a red flag and yelling, "Officer, come and get me. I'm driving under the influence."

One summer evening I watched a late model Ford driving at a reasonable clip north on Highway 33. I was about to pull out from a shopping center, where I had been checking the businesses. The last thing on my mind was a drunk driver. I was about to go for a cup of coffee when I saw the driver glance in my direction.

Without warning, the car veered off the road into a parking lot. The driver jumped out, walked around, and lifted the hood, then stood looking puzzled. Of course, being a conscientious officer, I stopped to assist.

Walking by the driver's side, I looked in and saw that the seat was wet. The odor of beer wafted from the interior. People who are drinking when they see a cop often panic and pour it all over the place, rather than just sticking the full can under the seat.

"What's the problem?" I asked.

"I don't know. It just died on me." His speech was slow and measured, the way speech is when you are making absolutely certain that you do not slur your words. He was a portly man of medium height, wearing casual, but expensive, clothes.

"Try to start it," I said.

"It's no use, officer. It's dead." He shrugged nervously as I stepped in close enough to smell the odor of beer on his breath.

"Humor me," I said with a smile. "Try it."

Reluctantly, the middle-aged man went back to the passenger compartment and turned the ignition. It fired right up, of course. "Well, how do you like that! Guess I'll be going on."

"No, sir, you won't. Turn off the ignition and step back outside. I'm going to give you a field sobriety test."

The first ploy having failed, he immediately launched into the second. A good cop can quote most of them verbatim.

"Officer, before this goes any further, I'd better warn you that I'm a substantial citizen in this county. It looks to me like you'd be out trying to prevent a few of these burglaries, rather than harassing taxpayers."

"That's what I was trying to do when you made an illegal turn in front of me, sir. Then, upon stopping to check on you, I couldn't help but notice that you reeked of an alcoholic beverage and had spilled beer all over your car."

"Honest to God, it just died." Any phrase that begins with an invocation of the deity will be followed by a lie.

"This test is really simple, but don't do anything until I tell you to. I'll demonstrate. I want you to lift one foot, then while balanced on that foot, recite the entire alphabet. A, B, C, D, E . . . all the way through to Z. You may begin."

Slowly and carefully the man balanced himself. "A, B, C, D, E, F . .." His other foot dropped. He balanced himself, then started again, "G, H. . .."

"Sorry, sir. That won't do. The idea is to recite the alphabet and remain balanced at the same time."

Angrily, but with determination, he started over. By the time he reached *H*, he was wobbling. When he got to *P*, he looked like a tightrope walker struggling for balance. He finished up, "T, U, Z, X, W, Y, and Z."

"There," he said triumphantly, barely preventing himself from toppling over as he finished, "how was *that?*"

"I seem to remember the alphabet in a different order. Now, I am going to hold up a pencil. I want you to focus on it. Follow the movement of the pencil, but *do not* move your head—only your eyes."

At close range, I saw that the man was even drunker than I had thought. His eyes fluttered wildly as he attempted to follow the movement of the pencil. This test is called the horizontal gaze nystagmus test. It was perfected by an eye doctor

197

who found that the eyes of an intoxicated person cannot move from side to side without jerking or fluttering. The alphabet test was merely a way of determining if he could do two things at once. An intoxicated person can only focus on one thing at a time.

"Sir, you are under arrest for driving under the influence of alcohol. Put your hands on the side of the car so I can pat you down."

"I will not! I am a respected member of this community. Someone might see me being searched as they pass. This is outrageous!"

"If you don't do as I say, they might see you being placed in a police car forcibly," I said quietly.

His shoulders slumped inside the tailored jacket he was wearing, but he complied.

"Now put your hands behind you."

"You're cuffing me for drunk driving?" His tone was incredulous.

"I cuff everyone that I arrest."

"This is ridiculous. I'm not a criminal!"

"The state disagrees, sir. Driving under the influence is not an optional arrest. I am required to take custody."

By the time I did the pull-in slip on his car and the inventory, he had slipped into the next predictable phase, which is remorse. I began my warrant and arrest report as we waited on the wrecker.

"Officer, I'm really sorry about this. I'm a community leader, chairman of the deacon board at my church. Can't we have someone pick me up? This is going to ruin my reputation."

"Baptist?" I asked.

"Why, yes." He brightened, thinking he had found a lever.

"It's always seemed peculiar to me, that 85 percent of this county professes to be Baptist or Methodist. Most Baptists equate alcoholic beverages with adultery, and the Methodist *Book of Discipline* condemns it. That other 15 percent sure buys a lot of beer."

"Oh, well," he sighed, "I know you're only doing your duty. I know you don't like to put people in jail."

"Wrong, sir. I'm quite proud to put people in jail. I can

sleep well later, knowing that you didn't kill yourself or anyone else before you got home."

"You sound a little self-righteous, my friend." His facade was slipping. I knew he would soon be indignant again and would probably tell me that he made more money in a month than I made in a year.

"No, sir, not self-righteous, just thorough. We both know this isn't the first time you've driven in this condition. This isn't the first time you've been stopped. You've been doing it long enough that you would fool an inexperienced patrolman. A nondrinker at your blood alcohol level would be nearly comatose."

"You won't know what my blood alcohol is until I have the test. When do I get the test, anyway? I don't appreciate your cavalier behavior."

"You'll get the test at the county jail. Your eyes told me just about what your blood alcohol level is. I teach other cops how to do it. Your blood alcohol is around .20 percent. You passed the legal level, which is twice what it ought to be, about six drinks back. Does that sound about right?" Later, he tested at .21 percent.

"Well, it just so happens you're wrong. I only had two beers!"

"Whatever you say, sir. By the way, jumping out to check under the hood is a dead giveaway."

29

"Knock, Knock, Knockin' on Heaven's Doors"

Americans always behave as if death is a surprise, as if it comes without warning and is an unusual event, not the destiny of every human being. Perhaps it is the same in every culture, but I can only speak for mine.

My first encounters with sudden death came, not as a cop, but as an ambulance driver in the late 1960s. One incident stands out in my mind.

The call seemed routine enough. An elderly man was lying on the bed, and his family could not wake him. My partner for that day, a plump, smiling young man (whom I will call Ed) and I pulled up in front of a modest frame house on the north side of Knoxville. Ed had just started work and had never ridden with me. After that day, I endeavored to see that he never worked with me again.

"Back here," a balding man of forty or so said as we went through the front door. It was a neat home, with lots of knick-knacks on the wall and on various tables. Many of the wall hangings were cross-stitch samplers. We passed through the kitchen, then into a middle bedroom where the man looked as if he had lain down for a nap—his last one. The skin of his cheek bones was drawn like parchment, his mouth open.

I checked the carotid artery for a pulse, the feel of cold human flesh sending chills up my spine as it always does. A living being feels alive; a dead person feels like a pack of meat under plastic. Still, I went through the motions, checking the pupils for movement.

"Go out to the ambulance and have the dispatcher send a homicide unit," I told Ed under my voice.

"Where's he goin'?" the man who had greeted us asked.

"Sir, I'm very sorry, but we got here too late to help your father." Ambulance attendants had to weigh their words carefully then. Only a doctor could make an official pronouncement of death.

"He'll be all right," the man said. "He's had these breathin' attacks before. Just give him some oxygen, and he'll be all right."

"No, sir, he will not be all right. He's been gone for several hours, at least. I know it's hard to accept, but that's the way it is."

"Are you a doctor?" he demanded.

"No, sir, but I go through this type of thing regularly." This was a Catch-22 situation. An ambulance attendant could not make a pronouncement of death, but, if a person was obviously dead, he could not move a body until the police examined it and got clearance from the coroner.

"Then, by God, you get him in that ambulance and take him to the hospital, right now!"

"I can't do that," I said. "It's against the law."

At that point, Ed strolled back into the house nonchalantly. "Dispatcher says the cop will be here in a few minutes."

"Cop?" the man said. "Oh, that's it. You think my daddy's drunk, and you want to have him arrested. Well, he ain't drunk, and you'd better get him to the hospital, now! You let my daddy die, and you won't live to talk about it!"

"Now, you listen to me," I snapped. "I'm sorry, but your father has passed away. I know it, and you know it. I understand that you're upset, but don't threaten me, or I'll get in that ambulance and leave until the police get here."

There was movement on the front porch. Three women, ranging from the late twenties to midthirties, walked up the front steps. The man went to meet them.

"What's wrong?" one of the women asked.

"Daddy's in there on the bed. Can't catch his breath, and

these ambulance bastards called the police. They won't take him to the hospital!"

Hearing the rustle of cellophane, then a crunching sound, I turned and saw that Ed had opened a pack of salad crackers from Shoneys and was munching away, as if he were on a picnic somewhere.

"That's some pretty needlework on that sampler up there. Did you see it?" Ed nodded at the wall above the bed. I stared in disbelief as the voices on the front porch grew louder.

The man stormed back into the house and confronted me again. "This is your last chance. Load my daddy in that ambulance, or I'll sue for everything you have."

"Look," I replied, biting off each word, "I am very sorry for what's happened, but I cannot move your father, not until the homicide officer arrives."

"Hey, Hunter. Look at this old jelly glass with the flowers on it. I haven't seen one of these in years." My partner was standing with a glass of water in his hand. He was washing down the crackers.

The man stalked back to the porch and huddled with his sisters again. I had seen denial before. It is a normal thing, but this was the first time I had ever seen anyone totally refuse to look at reality. I was becoming fearful that the situation was going to escalate to a physical confrontation. We were saved, however, as the unmarked cruiser pulled up in front of the house.

The four people ran to meet the puzzled homicide detective. "Officer, these ambulance people are lettin' our daddy die. Tell 'em to take him on and give him some oxygen," the man said.

Walking past them, without comment, the graying, chunky homicide officer came through the house, nodding at me. He laid his hand on the old man's arm.

"This guy's been dead for hours. What the hell's goin' on, Hunter?"

"They won't believe me. Maybe they'll believe you. I'd appreciate it if you'd hang around until we get him loaded."

"Sure, go ahead. I'll fill out my paperwork."

We went through the front door, pushing the sheet-covered body ahead of us, and started up the walk.

"He'll be all right, won't he, officer?" the man asked plaintively.

"Like the man's been tellin' you, he's dead. Been dead for hours. Now, I need some information."

Without a word or a sigh, the youngest of the women, a plump redhead, fell flat on her face, smashing her nose flat with a sound like an overripe melon. Before I could get to her, a second woman collapsed.

"Call for another crew," I told Ed. "That first one smashed her face on the sidewalk."

More relatives were arriving as we worked with the woman who had smashed her face. Two more went down. The son was telling everyone that we had let his father die. There was a great wailing, rising in volume with each moment. With two more units on the scene, I went to my ambulance with relief. As we pulled away, an adolescent boy of thirteen or fourteen ran up and slapped the passenger window with the flat of his hand.

"Murderers!" he screamed.

"What was *that* all about?" Ed asked, opening another pack of crackers.

"I have no idea, Ed. None at all. Just eat your crackers, and don't talk to me!"

"Damn, what did I do to make you so irritable?"

Two days later, when they had the funeral, three ambulances were dispatched to transport shock victims to the hospital. It was, to be sure, an extreme illustration, but the denial was typical.

A few years ago, I happened on the scene of a head-on collision in the early hours of a Sunday morning. Pulling up, I called for a rescue team and ambulances.

"Do you know CPR?" a young man screamed in my face. The youth's eyes were wild, and I smelled alcoholic beverage on his breath. Pushing past him, I crawled through the rear window of the crumpled car, then over the front seat.

There was a young man, blond, husky, neatly dressed. He was still upright in the seat, head forward. Blood had trickled from his nose, staining the light colored pants he wore. Once again, I smelled the odor of an alcoholic beverage as I checked him for signs of life. There were none.

After crawling back out of the wreckage, I started toward the other vehicle to see if there was anything I could do.

The first young man blocked my way and grabbed my shoulders. "Start CPR! You can bring my friend back. I've seen it in the movies!" There were tears on his face. His hair was hanging in stringy curls.

"I can't bring your friend back. I'm sorry, but I may be able to help the other driver."

"You *will* start CPR! You'll do it, now! *Bring him back!*" Two husky civilians stepped forward and restrained him while I checked on the second driver, who was seriously injured, but conscious.

Eventually, he had to be placed in a cruiser until his family arrived. Later, I would put together a story of heavy drinking and a celebration that turned into a wake. Months later, the young man was still telling anyone who would listen that his friend died because the cop "wouldn't give him CPR."

It was understandable, I suppose. Nothing in his existence had prepared him for what had happened. Death, he had been taught, is something that happens to old people in hospitals or to fictional characters.

Look how beautifully Ali McGraw died in *Love Story*. Watch the television and movie cowboys die, still talking right up to the end and having a final cigarette. Young friends are not supposed to die, drunk and in a twisted car with scarlet blood trickling from their nostrils and pink foam dripping from their lips.

I have seen them die too often and have looked into their eyes as they took a final breath. The worst are the violent, senseless deaths you encounter along the way: a teenager stabbed to death over which record to play next; a young husband shot to death because he was teasing the dog; a man bleeding to death from gunshots over a card game with less than twenty dollars on the table; two children crumpled and broken on the pavement, victims of a drunk driver. There is no pattern, rhyme, or reason.

We stand in shock at funeral homes and say, "It was so *sudden*." We forget that it was scripted into the genes at the moment of conception. Our literature tells us that. Our Bible tells us that. But we deny it.

When I was a boy, my father used to have a favorite ending

205

to the prayers that he prayed. A convert from Catholicism to the Fundamentalism of the Southern Baptist church, he never doubted that God was listening.

"Heavenly Father," he would say, "when you have finished with me, grant me a peaceful and happy hour in which to die."

A heart damaged from birth struck him down at forty. A stroke followed, paralyzing him on the left side. The doctors said he was finished and would die in his bed. He went on praying, though, and working until he was walking and moving under his own power. The doctor would shake his head in amazement when my father walked into his office.

He nagged the doctor to let him drive again. He could no longer be an ironworker, but he intended to do something. Finally, the doctor said he would release him to drive on the next visit.

With the slight limp left from the stroke, he began his preparations. He cleaned out the garage for an "antique business" and scoured the storage shed for items to sell. The morning of the doctor's appointment, he stood at the bathroom sink, shaving and joking with my brother. He felt good, knowing that he was about to be mobile again. He turned, as if to speak, and went over in my brother's arms. He was gone, felled by a massive cerebral hemorrhage.

At the age of twenty, I had no concept of how young forty-one really is. Looking back, I have come to understand. "Forty," an old saying goes, "is the old age of youth and the youth of old age."

There has never been a doubt in my mind that the God my father served granted his prayer. My father died in a happy hour, and with his family—not looking back, but looking forward—without regrets, and with hope.

Death is a certainty. Cops know it well. One day we will all, as Bob Dylan's song says, be "Knock, knock, knockin' on heaven's doors."

Personally, I hope to be ready.

30

Nothing Good Happens at Three in the Morning

It was the dead hour, three o'clock in the morning, the time when cops drink too much coffee and think too much. Every street cop knows that nothing good happens at three in the morning.

The dispatcher sent a beat car to check on a possible "dead body in the road." I was near, so I headed that way to back the officer up in case it turned out to be genuine. Most such calls are the figment of overactive imaginations and eyes strained by too many hours on the road. A dead dog, an unfortunate 'possum, or even the recap from an old tire becomes a "dead body."

Also, I was one of the few photographers on the road at that time. Now there are many, but then few had been trained. It was, and is, policy to photograph fatal accidents whenever feasible.

Ahead of me on the concrete highway were blue, red, and amber lights bouncing in a kaleidoscopic pattern off cars and spectators, from the police cruiser, the ambulance, the fire truck, and a wrecker.

Walking past the other emergency vehicles, I saw that this was no figment of imagination but the stuff of nightmares. I could tell it by the strained, stiff manner in which the ambulance crew was standing. There was a creature on the pavement that maintained enough of the basic shape of a human being to make us understand what we were seeing.

A totally dismembered human being will make you swallow hard, perhaps even take a deep breath. Total dismemberment, however, turns a body into an abstract puzzle. What we saw that night makes you immediately fight back the bile and gag reflex. Fresh blood has a distinct, though unexplainable, odor. Steam from the warm body wafted in the cold air, hanging over the scene, as if life were reluctant to depart hurriedly.

Half the face remained. Brains spilled out the other side of the head, leaving an eye nestled in the gray matter. The cloth of a shirt or blouse was interwoven with muscle, sinew, and bone. It was a young male, or a female; we could not tell. The hair remaining was nearly shoulder length, but that means nothing today. Males and females wear loafers and blue jeans.

The ambulance attendants shook out a clean white sheet over the remains and it softly floated down, covering the horror. We all were wearing masks that night, pretending that it was just another routine call. Professionals do not admit to shock and revulsion.

"The car's down here," the beat officer said, pointing down in a field. I got my camera bag and we walked down to the vehicle. There was very little damage. The injuries to the deceased had not happened inside the vehicle.

"Seat belt would have made the difference," the beat officer said. He was a tall man, young, but used to horror. I shot pictures as he collected his information.

"From what I can see here, the victim was thrown from the car and was either run over by another vehicle or dragged by this car."

I nodded, my mind on the task still ahead. The pictures had to be made. I would have to get close, very close, to focus in. It was not something to look forward to.

We made the measurements for the report, pulling a steel tape along the skid marks as if it were an ordinary fender-bender. When we were finished, I walked back to the body and unslung my camera.

"Officer?"

Turning, I found a young man with his arm extended, holding a leather wallet. He was holding it gingerly between two fingers. It was soaked on one side with blood.

"I found this over by the guardrail."

Opening the wallet, I found the operator's license in the front panel. The young man who smiled at me from behind the plastic cover bore no resemblance to the nightmare he had become. I handed the wallet to the beat officer and nodded for the ambulance crew to remove the sheet.

"Somebody shine a light on him so I can focus my camera," I said. The horror now had a sex and a name.

Kneeling, I focused on the details of his shirt pattern, refusing to look at the entire frame. That makes it manageable—not a person but a detail. The strobe flashed eerily, momentarily blanking out the colored lights.

One of the great horrors of my life is that the things I have seen will one day burst past the dam I have built to keep them away, flooding me with all the terrible things I refused to look at, even when they were in front of me.

"You can move him," I said, finishing as quickly as possible.

The ambulance crew rolled him onto a rubber sheet. Before closing it, they searched the area, returning with skull fragments and teeth. One crew member used a stiff sheet of cardboard to scrape up gray matter.

When the body was moved, a fire engine started up and a section of hose was unrolled. A fireman began to wash down the concrete, and gum wrappers, cigarette butts, blood, and fragments of flesh were pushed ahead of the foaming spray.

"Hunter, would you mind closing down the traffic for a few minutes until the wrecker can get the car out?"

"Sure."

Walking back to my cruiser, I ignored the curious faces peering from the passing cars. Opening the trunk, I stored my camera equipment, got into the car, and blocked both lanes. Even at that time of morning, traffic quickly began to back up.

On my log sheet, I noted that I had assisted at the scene of an automobile accident. It seemed stark, as do all police reports, telling the story but really telling nothing.

The door opened on a new Buick about three cars back, and a middle-aged woman stalked toward me.

"Officer, how long can we expect to be tied up here?"

"There's been a fatal accident. We're cleaning up the highway." Usually, the mention of a fatality will cause people to say, "Oh, I'm sorry," and quickly depart. This woman was of a different breed.

"That's unfortunate," she said, hands on hips, "but the rest of us still have places to go." I noticed that the steam from her breath hung in the air around her, like the steam from the still-warm body.

"Lady, go get in your car. We will open the lanes as soon as possible."

"I don't think I like your attitude. Give me your badge number. We'll see if your superiors appreciate your tone of voice!"

She apparently expected me to collapse in terror at the demand for my badge number. I got out of the cruiser, fishing a card from my shirt pocket.

"Here's a card with my badge number and my name. Make sure you spell it properly when you complain. Now, go get in your car as I told you before I place you under arrest for failing to obey a lawful order from a police officer. *Now!*" She stalked back to the new Buick indignantly, large buttocks wiggling obscenely.

A few minutes later, the beat officer radioed me to open the lanes. I did so, pulling over on the shoulder. The woman in the Buick made an obscene gesture at me as she passed. I saw that the new Buick had a taillight out, and momentarily I considered a citation for her husband, then decided not.

I was tired. It was almost time to go home.

A few minutes later, I stopped for one more cup of coffee. The Merita Bread salesman came into the market carrying his wares. We often saw each other out on his beat and mine.

"Anything interesting happen last night?" he asked.

"No, it was pretty slow," I replied, having no desire at all to talk about the remains of a young man being washed down the drain with cigarette butts and gum wrappers.

31

A Minor Disturbance

Cruising Emory Road, my shift almost over for the night, I saw a cruiser pull into an all-night market that is popular with officers. Turning into the lot, I watched my brother get out of the driver's side. A rookie named Bill McKee climbed out the passenger side. A big man with a fierce mustache, I saw that he towered over Larry who, like me, barely hits five feet, six inches.

"What's going on?" my brother asked.

"Nothing much. I have some comp time coming. Thought I'd go home early tonight."

"Let's drink a cup first," he said.

As we approached the door of the market, a jeep-type vehicle pulled in. A worried looking woman got out and called out to the two uniformed officers. They spoke to her as I went in and ordered coffee with double cream and sugar. In the morning my coffee is black and hot. At other times, sweet and warm.

Walking out the door, I saw that the woman had gotten back into the vehicle. I looked at my brother questioningly. He shrugged.

"Domestic dispute," he said. "The woman lives across the county line. She says her sister called earlier and said her husband was threatening her life. He's supposed to have several weapons."

"Long guns or handguns?"

"She thinks they're all long guns, but she isn't sure. Let's go have a look. It's been a while since she talked to her sister. Maybe the guy has passed out by now."

"Where is it?" I asked.

He named a trailer park where we had both been many times.

"I told them to pull in at the shopping center and to stay there no matter what happens until an officer comes to get them," my brother said.

"I'll go with you," I told him. Larry nodded, without speaking. I know, because I feel the same way, that having your brother with you in a combat situation adds an extra element of worry. He did not argue, though. He knew that I would go, regardless of what he said, just as he would go with me.

"We'll be more than glad to have you," McKee said. Bill is a solid man. I had watched him working in the jail for the last couple of years. To him I am an old-timer, a survivor. It always makes a rookie glad to have old-timers around. The veterans have learned to control the appearance of fear. He had no way of knowing that my stomach was churning and my breath already accelerating.

Alcohol, a family dispute, and weapons are always a deadly combination waiting to explode with fatal results. I threw the cup of coffee into a garbage can, having learned through the years that if you take a cup of coffee on a hot call, it will always end up in your lap.

I have been lucky through the years. None of my hundreds of domestic disputes have ever ended fatally. I cannot begin to remember, however, how many times tragedy has been averted by an alert officer who noticed a weapon before the suspect had time to use it.

As I followed Larry's cruiser down Emory Road, memories came back. Now I am an investigator, and this beat belongs to someone else. But it was mine for a long time, and I know it like the back of my hand—all the nooks, crannies, and secret places.

I knew the place where we were headed because I had spent a lot of my street career there. Most trailer parks are inhabited by people who are passing through. There will be another family the next time you go.

At a shopping center parking lot, my brother pulled in and again instructed the people in the car to wait until one of us returned for them. A cop does not want or need civilians wandering into a combat zone. As we headed to our destination, Larry informed the dispatcher of our location in case we had something we could not handle.

We killed our lights and coasted down the long driveway, our tires crunching on the coarse gravel. The residence was lit up. I thought of training sessions. The "book" would tell us to call in several more units and surround the house like a military operation.

Patrolmen laugh a lot about "textbook" operations. If everything was done "by the book," they know, nothing would ever get done. There are simply too many calls in the course of a week.

We got out of our cruisers and approached, eyes riveted on the doors and windows. We had not made much noise, but we might have been heard. Moving from cover to cover (a parked car, a tree, or whatever was available), we approached the front of the residence.

Voices filtered through the windows and doors—male and female. The suspect was still awake, not passed out. Weapons in hand, Larry and Bill McKee flattened out on each side of the door. Standing back about fifteen feet and to the side, I stood with my pistol leveled at the door and the windows on each side. If someone fired from inside, I would be able to take them out, I hoped.

Larry reached across and knocked on the door. It was the moment of truth. In the next instant, gunfire might erupt from inside. Tensed, we waited.

The door opened almost immediately. A tiny, blond woman, with a tear-streaked face and stringy hair, opened the door. Terror was written on her face. Visible behind her was a large man with his back partially turned. The expression on the woman's face told the story.

Without alerting the man, Larry and McKee stepped past the woman. As they did so, the man turned, a startled expression on his face. "Police. Don't move from where you're standing!" Larry yelled.

The man turned and darted toward an open door. His movement was purposeful; he was not fleeing but going for a

213

weapon. We were all moving at once. Larry slammed into the big man with his shoulder as the man reached out, bouncing him off the wall and toppling him backward. His momentum carried both him and the suspect over a coffee table, slamming them onto a couch.

Holstering my weapon as I went, I jumped and touched down on the table as I hurled myself into the fray. By that time, McKee had one of the man's arms, Larry another. Reaching around his neck as he struggled grimly, I locked in under his ear and began to apply pressure. The pain from such a move is excruciating. I know from experience.

"Stop fighting, or I'll hurt you," I hissed.

Moments later the man went limp. The cuffs were locked down, and McKee and I hoisted the big man to his feet. "What's this all about?" the man asked, but got no answer. We were all gasping for breath.

Turning to the door where he had been headed, Larry began to remove weapons, three of them: a .12-gauge shotgun, a .30–.06 rifle, and a .22 caliber rifle. All were semiautomatic.

"You meant to shoot someone, didn't you, pal?" Larry asked, his face flushed. "Take him out while I talk to his wife."

"I ain't goin' nowhere. I ain't done nothin'," the big man said.

"Easy or hard, macho man," I told him. "We all weigh more than ninety pounds." The adrenaline was still pumping.

"So does she," the man sobbed. "She weighs about a hundred and twenty." He seemed to think the distinction was important.

A few minutes later, the prisoner loaded and being watched by McKee, I went back inside. The woman was sitting at the kitchen table sobbing. She told a story of being held at gunpoint and threatened for hours.

"There's a number on this card," my brother said as he laid it on the table. "Call in the morning. The lady who answers is a woman's advocate. She was a battered wife and is a former police officer. She'll tell you what you need to do."

"Will he be able to make bond tonight?" she asked, tears running freely.

"If he can get the money. Your sister is down the road. You need to get a few belongings together. This officer will drive you down to your sister's car. The advocate will tell you how to get the rest of your stuff."

"I can't believe he did this," she sobbed.

"Come on," I said, "this is not the first time he's been violent with you."

"No. He's punched me and jerked me around, but he never threatened my life before."

"Well, it won't get any better," my brother said. "I know from experience. Your husband has severe emotional problems. He's dangerous."

We carried the woman's belongings to my car. As we passed the other cruiser, the man tried to yell at his wife. McKee opened the door and told him to be quiet. After that, he sat in sullen silence.

As I pulled from the driveway, heading back to the shopping center, the jeep-type vehicle came up toward the driveway. The woman's sister and brother-in-law got out, eyes wide.

"I thought you were told to stay at the shopping center until one of us came back," I growled as they approached my car.

"The officer told us, but . . ."

"If you had pulled in at the wrong time, someone could have been killed! The next time, listen!" At such times, innocent-eyed civilians anger an officer. The adrenaline in my system was still raging.

"I'm sorry," the sister said.

"You'll receive a subpoena," I told the victim, "and your testimony will be crucial. Your husband will try to talk you out of it. If you don't prosecute, this was all for nothing."

"I'll prosecute," she said firmly.

Heading home, I noticed for the first time that my shoulder was throbbing. In the movies, middle-aged officers carry out tremendous physical feats. In real life, forty-year-old cops pull muscles and tendons, as I had done. It was two weeks before full use returned to my shoulder.

I made a vow to stay away from patrol calls. It is, after all, not my job any longer. Two nights later, though, I found myself backing up another patrol unit, this time with one practically useless arm. Fortunately, it came to nothing. A good cop always reacts to a hot call the way a beagle reacts to a rabbit.

"Well, the hearing's over on the guy with the three weapons," my brother said over the telephone. A conflicting case had put me in another court that day.

"Did it go to the grand jury?"

"Nope. The 'aggravated assault' was reduced to 'simple assault.' He was put on probation."

"Why?" I asked, indignation rising.

"His wife was with him. They were all lovey-dovey. She said the matter was not as serious as we indicated. The attorney general had no choice but to reduce it. She wasn't going to testify against him."

"Let's just hope one of us is working when she calls for help again," I raged. "Let's see if she can get us to risk our lives the next time. There'll be a next time, you know!"

"I know," Larry replied quietly. He had calmed down and was taking it philosophically. Such things happen to patrolmen every day. I had been away for a while.

Later, after I had calmed down, I thought the matter through. When the woman called again, we would all go. We are cops, under oath to protect and serve. We would do the same thing we did the last time, and probably with the same results.

After all, when the adrenaline stops flowing, in the calm atmosphere of a courtroom it will be viewed as just another minor disturbance, not a situation in which armed men confront each other and life and death decisions must be made on a moment's notice.

32

The Man Who Learned His Lesson

Cruising south on I–75, I listened to my prisoner as he rambled on in a drunken, disjointed manner. It was an ordinary Saturday night, or rather, early Sunday morning.

"It's the las' time I try to help a frien'. I can tell you that. I'm gonna be hard and cruel from now on, and you're responsible. I get outta bed to go after somebody who's too drunk to drive, an' what happens? You arres' me for drunk drivin'. Is that right? I ask you, is that right?"

He was a scrawny man of thirty or so wearing gold-rimmed glasses. Nobody had told him that his shaggy, shoulder-length hair went out of style years ago. The excuse he was offering is a common one: "I was trying to be a Good Samaritan, so I deserve mercy."

"I didn't arrest you for being a good citizen," I answered. "I arrested you for driving under the influence of an alcoholic beverage. I don't know how drunk your friend is, but he probably is more sober than you."

"I guess you never broke the law. Right? I guess you're mister perfect."

"*My God!*" The words escaped me involuntarily as a northbound car barely missed hitting me head-on. It took me a second to realize the full horror of the situation. He was going the wrong way—*north*bound in the *south*bound lane! The traffic at that time of the morning was still fairly heavy.

It only took me a few seconds to sort things out and make a decision. The prisoner in the back of my cruiser was my responsibility, but weighed against the car hurtling the wrong way on the interstate, his well being and mine had become secondary. I had to warn the oncoming traffic.

"You'll never catch him," the drunk in my back seat giggled. "He was goin' too fast."

Wheeling on the shoulder in a long curve, I turned. With all emergency equipment running wide open, I gunned down the interstate, attempting to overtake the vehicle. With horns blowing in anger and fear, oncoming cars began to drive on the shoulders and the median, narrowly averting disaster.

In a few minutes I was on his bumper, screaming at him over the public address system. A recording of the things I was yelling at him probably would have scorched the ears of the innocent. I do not remember. All I can recall was the terror of wondering if I would ever see my family again. It also was not lost on me how I would look in the newspaper if anyone were killed in this encounter. I would look like a hotdog who had ignored every safety rule he had ever been taught.

Weaving from one side of the road to the other, he continued on, seemingly unaware of lights, siren, and curses coming from behind. Suddenly and without warning, he turned up a southbound exit ramp. Still going the wrong way, he was nonetheless off the main road.

I decided to overtake and ram him, if necessary. Ramming a vehicle is all right on television, but real police administrators do not tolerate it. Fortunately, I was spared the decision. Turning off the exit ramp, he drove into a railroad underpass in a crescendo of screaming metal.

"Kill that sonofabitch!" my prisoner screamed from the back, his relaxed manner now gone. Glancing at him, I saw that his feet were braced against the screen and his eyes were still wide with terror from his involuntary chase. He looked almost sober. Fear will perk you up.

Killing the driver may have been exactly what I had in mind as I charged the car, adrenaline pumping and not even considering that he might be armed. All I wanted to do was get my hands on him. Jerking the door open, I caught him by the shoulders and half lifted, half threw him out of the vehicle. He was a big fellow, and his legs were like rubber. There was no fight. It took all my energy to keep him from smashing his face on the ground.

Back-up units from the city police were on the scene in moments. After they took the prisoner off my hands, I leaned against the car, breathing hard and trying to regain control. It is unspent adrenaline that kills cops.

"Hey," one of the city officers yelled, "here's a baggie and an empty half-pint bottle. He's been drinkin' and smokin' wacky weed."

The crowd in front of general sessions court ebbed and flowed, as it does every weekday afternoon. Civil cases are heard in the morning; all others begin at 1:30 P.M. There is always a nervousness about the crowd; men and women are going to judgment.

They are all mixed together in sessions court, which is the bottom level court in Tennessee: whores, drunks, those who have assaulted and been assaulted, citizens on minor traffic violations. They all mingle. Even serious felonies are first heard in sessions court. A judge in this court can only pass sentences on misdemeanors, but it is also the place where "probable cause" hearings are heard. Some serious felonies end here by dismissal.

While the suspects are waiting nervously in front of the courtroom, cops and lawyers are in the hallway behind the courtroom. Some will be waiting on a judge to sign a warrant or an order, but most are there to try a case, either as prosecutor or defense lawyer. They talk, laugh, smoke, bitch, and make deals.

There are too many cases for them all to be tried. Plea bargaining starts in the hallway behind the courtroom. Everyone—cops, the attorney general, defense lawyers, judges—knows that most cases must be plea bargained, or the system will break down.

Strictly speaking, to prosecute or not to prosecute—to deal or not to deal—is the province of the attorney general or his assistants. In reality, though, many plea bargains are worked out by cops and defense attorneys. The attorney general's office tries to maintain a good relationship with the cops who ply their trade there.

There are two main reasons for cops and prosecutors to get along: they must work together and they do generally respect each other. A good assistant attorney general will seldom deal on a case if the officer has reason to be adamant about prosecuting. Maybe the officer was hurt or had problems with the suspect. They try to work together.

So the defense attorneys (if they are wise and experienced) go to cops first, knowing that an angry cop may blow up and cause problems at what he considers an unjust deal. If the cop buys a plea bargain, the assistant attorney general will usually go along with it, and vice versa.

"Officer Hunter, how are you today?" The lawyer extended his hand, smiling. I took it and returned the smile. He is a man I like. He fights hard for his clients but understands that they may not be telling him the entire truth. A big man with a shock of blond hair, he genuinely likes cops.

"John Walters," I replied. "I'm fine. How are you?"

"Can't complain. Catching many fish this year?" he asked with a chuckle, knowing that I am a man who seldom goes out of the house except when forced. He is an avid sportsman.

"I'm afraid not, John. All right, which one is it? I know you're not here because you love this place."

"You wound me, Hunter, to suggest an ulterior motive to my overtures of friendship. However . . ." he let his voice trail off. "I would like to speak to you about a Michael Burgin."

"Forget it, John. He either pleads guilty on all charges and takes his chances, or it goes to criminal court."

"Let's not be hasty, now. Sometimes there are mitigating circumstances. His blood alcohol level was only .09 percent, and there was barely enough marijuana for a test."

"Don't lay that crap on me, John. There was only a little marijuana left because he had smoked the entire bag. He would have still been falling down drunk, even if he hadn't been drinking."

"We freely admit that he was intoxicated beyond all reasonable doubt."

"Well, I'm glad you're being magnanimous about it. So, why are you trying to make a deal, then?"

"What did his criminal history look like?"

"We both know it was clean. But that just means he hadn't been caught before. He drove a car down the wrong side of the interstate endangering numerous people, including me."

"Guilty," John said, "and ready to pay a hefty fine, attend a rehabilitation program, do public service, and even go to jail, if necessary. Being the compassionate man you are, though, when you hear the story, you'll ask the judge to have mercy on him."

"All right. Lay on me this tale of woe—but it won't matter. I'm still very upset."

"To begin with, it was the first time my client had ever smoked marijuana or drunk alcohol. He grew up in a strict religious environment, married his childhood sweetheart, and has two children. He went to work for the firm with which he is now employed right out of high school, eight years ago.

"The night you arrested him, he went home and found out his wife had run off with another man. He just went all to pieces, drove down to the strip, and tried to put himself to sleep. With only a high school education, he'll never get another job like the one he has. A conviction for drunk driving will destroy the rest of his life."

"That's the most ludicrous story I ever heard. If it were true, though, what did you have in mind?"

"My client will attend drug and alcohol rehabilitation, do thirty days of public service work, plead guilty, be placed on diversion, and at the end of the year, have all charges dismissed."

"Bull. He committed a serious crime, and he deserves whatever he gets."

"Hunter, do you arrest people to punish them or to make sure they don't do it again?"

"Both," I replied honestly.

"If I can convince you that he has not only learned a lesson, but has suffered immensely, will you go along with it?"

"Sure, but there's no way you're going to do that."

"Can you describe my client?"

"Of course. He's about six feet, maybe 220, blond, mid to late twenties."

"Come over here to the door." We walked down the hall so that we could see the lobby.

"Do you see the man you arrested?" John asked.

"No. He's not out there."

"Try the guy in the baggy blue suit."

"Nope. That guy can't weigh more than 150 pounds. The guy I arrested was a big, strapping boy."

"That's him. He's lost nearly seventy pounds. Watch him. He has a twitch in his jaw. He has literally worried himself into that state. I don't think he'll ever break the law again."

"You're kidding, right? He has cancer or something."

"No. It was strictly worry and remorse. How about it? His fate is in your hands. You can finish him off, or give him another chance."

Five years after the incident, I saw my prisoner's picture in the newspaper. He had just been elected president of a civic group. The paper went on to tell of his other community achievements and talked about his wife and family. Presumably, they got back together.

Most stories about drunk drivers do not end this way. I am glad, though, that it happens from time to time. It would be sad to think that there are never any happy endings.

My job is to protect and serve. I took an oath to do just that, but a little mercy never hurts. It takes the edge off the cynicism.

I am glad I did it. And I am glad he made it. He was, indeed, a man who learned his lesson.

Epilogue

Writing a book is a little like standing naked in a public place. Once you have exposed yourself to the world at large, you must endure the world's opinion and comments.

To show emotion is human. Unfortunately, literature and dramatic art have put upon men in general, and cops in particular, a burden too heavy to be borne. The legend of strong, silent heroes, enduring silently, shapes the public's image of the men and women who carry badges.

A cinematic cop kills a couple of criminals, makes a sneering comment, then goes about the business of being strong, efficient, and emotionless.

When real cops kill people, it is not good drama. Real cops cry, tremble, sometimes throw up, and maybe go into shock. Some pray for forgiveness. Most spend a lot of time wondering if there was anything they could have done that would have prevented the death.

Many are finished with police work, emotionally destroyed at having taken a human life. They can tell you to the last detail about the blood frothing from the lips of a dying suspect and how he wheezed and gasped for breath the night they pulled the trigger.

Still, when I began to write, I wondered how flesh and blood cops would respond to books that paint them as less than heroic figures. How would they respond to me when I stood up and told the world that I cry when I'm sad and shake with fear when I'm frightened?

I need not have worried.

My friends, of course, were supportive, as friends are, when *The Moon Is Always Full* was published. The calls I received from civilians were overwhelmingly positive. They thanked me for showing them that cops are as human as everyone else.

It was an old street cop, though, who finally convinced me that I had done what I set out to do: write about cops as they are, not as they are portrayed on television and the movies.

When he showed up at my office door, my book was the last thing I expected to talk about. He limped in, a veteran cop recovering from his last injury, a man who was patrolling the streets a decade before I pinned on a badge.

I greeted him, then waited for him to state his business. There was a night many years ago when he had given me a royal tongue lashing for what he called "a stupid, rookie, cowboy stunt." Guilty as accused, I did not talk back. He shifted uncomfortably in front of my desk, before speaking.

"I read your book. You done good, Hunter. And I think you're a good cop."

He spun and limped away before I could recover enough to speak. The man of action, who had probably never been in a bookstore before he went looking for my book, had left the man of words with nothing to say.

The opinion of one battered, tough, cynical old street cop vindicated my work as no book critic ever will.

He will be out there putting his body in the path of evil, touching the untouchable, seeing the unthinkable, whether anyone says thanks or not. That is what he does. Somebody, though, needs to tell his story, and I intend to do it.

As long as the stories continue to come.